OFF THE GROUND
AN ANTHOLOGY OF POETRY

Compiled by

ALEXANDER HADDOW, B.A.
LATE
PRINCIPAL MASTER OF METHOD, THE TRAINING COLLEGE, GLASGOW
Author of "On the Teaching of Poetry" and "The Ring and the Book as a Connected Narrative"

and

WILLIAM KERR, M.A.
LATE
DIRECTOR OF STUDIES, THE TRAINING COLLEGE, GLASGOW
Author of "The English Apprentice"

BOOK III

Granger Index Reprint Series

BOOKS FOR LIBRARIES PRESS
FREEPORT, NEW YORK

© ALEXANDER HADDOW AND WILLIAM KERR, 1936
BOOKS FOR LIBRARIES EDITION 1969

STANDARD BOOK NUMBER:
8369-6067-X

LIBRARY OF CONGRESS CATALOG CARD NUMBER:
76-75516

PREFACE

"Poesy only instructs as it delights."—*John Dryden*.

"The end of writing is to instruct; the end of poetry is to instruct by pleasing."—*Samuel Johnson*.

Those sentences, we hope, are an indication at once of the purpose and the plan of this anthology. In making it we have been guided by one consideration—the aesthetic value of each poem for the readers we have in view. Of our notes we would merely say what will be immediately obvious, that we have made no attempt to construct lessons. We believe, indeed, that for every poem taught many should be read aloud, and that very often a beautiful and sympathetic reading will teach more than all the commentators. Naturally, therefore, we hold that no book can take the place of the teacher, whose ultimate aim is to lead pupils to enjoy reading poetry for themselves.

We wish to thank all who have so generously assisted us, especially Mr. A. D. Campbell, M.A., whose expert knowledge of proof-reading has been invaluable.

A. H.
W. K.

Our method of collaboration is that each undertakes a book, relying upon the other for all the help and encouragement that criticism and suggestion can give. The final responsibility for this book is mine.

A. H.

ACKNOWLEDGMENTS

We value highly the permission to include copyright material in this anthology, and are happy to put on record our indebtedness for :

"Treasure Trove," to Miss Marion Angus, and Messrs. Faber and Faber, publishers of " The Turn of the Day."

"The Little Dancers," to Mr. Laurence Binyon.

"London Snow," to the Clarendon Press, publishers of " The Shorter Poems of Robert Bridges," 1931.

"Hervé Riel," to Mr. John Murray.

"The Golden Journey to Samarkand," to Messrs. Martin Secker, Ltd., publishers of " The Collected Poems of James Elroy Flecker."

"The Parrots," to Mr. W. W. Gibson, and Messrs. Macmillan & Co., Ltd., publishers of " Collected Poems, 1905-1925."

"Ducks," to Mr. F. W. Harvey and Messrs. Sidgwick & Jackson, Ltd., publishers of " Ducks, and other Verses."

"The Yerl o' Waterydeck," to Dr. Greville MacDonald and Messrs. Chatto and Windus, publishers of " The Complete Poetical Works of George MacDonald."

"Silver " and " The Listeners," to Mr. Walter de la Mare.

"A Ballad of Cape St. Vincent," and

"The Golden City of St. Mary," reprinted from " Collected Poems " (Heinemann) by permission of Mr. John Masefield.

"Overheard on a Saltmarsh," from " Children of Love," published by The Poetry Bookshop.

Extract from " The Bacchae," to Professor Gilbert Murray and Messrs. Allen and Unwin, Ltd.

"San Stefano, a Ballad of the Bold Menelaus," to Sir Henry Newbolt, and Mr. John Murray, publisher of " Poems New and Old."

"The Highwayman," to Mr. Alfred Noyes and Messrs. William Blackwood & Sons, Ltd., publishers of " Collected Poems."

"The Raiders," to Mr. Will H. Ogilvie.

"A Piper," to Mr. Seumas O'Sullivan.

"The Ship," to Sir John C. Squire and Messrs. William Heinemann, Ltd.

"The Vagabond," " A Camp " and " I Will Make You Brooches," to Messrs. Chatto & Windus.

Extract from " Kidnapped," to Mr. Lloyd Osbourne and Messrs. Cassell & Co., Ltd.

"The Revenge," to the Author's Representatives, and Messrs. Macmillan & Co., Ltd.

"Two Pewits," to Messrs. Ingpen & Grant, publishers of " Collected Poems of Edward Thomas."

We have taken the liberty of including " The Stranger " by A. Muir, and express our indebtedness to the Author, whom we have been unable to trace.

CONTENTS

	PAGES	
	POEM	NOTES
San Stefano	11	165
The Splendour Falls on Castle Walls	14	165
Piping down the Valleys Wild	15	166
The Listeners	16	166
Overheard on a Saltmarsh	18	168
Treasure-Trove	19	168
The Forsaken Merman	20	168
Kilmeny	26	169
Thomas the Rhymer	29	170
La Belle Dame sans Merci	34	—
Morte D'Arthur	36	170
Le Morte D'Arthur	38	170
Autolycus' Songs	41	171
The Stranger	42	171
For A' That, and A' That	43	172
The Vagabond	45	172
A Camp	46	172
From "As You Like It"	47	173
I Will Make You Brooches	51	174
Pictures from "I Stood Tiptoe upon a Little Hill"	52	175
The Dowie Dens o' Yarrow	53	175
Sir Patrick Spens	57	176
The Shipwreck	61	177
The Bonnie Earl of Murray (*First Version*)	62	177
The Bonnie Earl of Murray (*Second Version*)	63	177
A Piper	65	178
The Little Dancers	66	179

CONTENTS—*continued*

	POEM	NOTES
The Contest in Music	67	180
Orpheus	72	181
From "The Merchant of Venice"	73	—
From "A Chorus of Euripides"	74	—
Reverie of Poor Susan	75	181
Westminster Bridge	76	181
London Snow	77	182
When Icicles Hang by the Wall	79	182
From "Frost at Midnight"	80	183
The Parrots	81	183
Two Pewits	82	184
Ducks	83	185
The Skylark	86	185
To a Skylark	87	185
The Tiger	88	186
Hervé Riel	89	186
Lucy Ashton's Song	96	187
The Reply	96	187
The Yerl o' Waterydeck	97	187
From "The Tempest"	103	187
Open the Door to Me, Oh!	104	188
To Althea from Prison	105	188
Mary Morison	107	188
The Highwayman	108	189
Silver	114	189
Some Moon Pictures from the Poets	115	190
The Raiders	118	190
Sir William of Deloraine	120	—
The Foray	121	190
The War Song of Dinas Vawr	122	191
Macpherson's Farewell	124	191
Pibroch of Donuil Dhu	126	191

CONTENTS—*continued*

	POEM	NOTES
Harlaw	128	192
The Vision of Belshazzar	130	192
David's Lament for Jonathan	132	193
Incident of the French Camp	133	193
Boot and Saddle	135	193
Will Ye No Come Back Again?	136	194
Bonnie Prince Charlie	137	194
Home Thoughts from the Sea	138	194
A Ballad of Cape St. Vincent	139	194
How Sleep the Brave	141	195
The Revenge	142	195
The Fight about the Isles of Açores	149	195
The Golden City of St. Mary	152	196
My Lost Youth	153	196
Songs from "The Tempest"	154	197
Pictures from Shakespeare	156	—
Call for the Robin Redbreast and the Wren	158	197
The Golden Journey to Samarkand	159	197
The Ship	163	198

INDEX OF AUTHORS

		Page
ANONYMOUS	Sir Patrick Spens	57
	The Bonnie Earl of Murray	62
	The Dowie Dens o' Yarrow	53
	Thomas the Rhymer	29
ANGUS, MARION	Treasure Trove	19
ARNOLD, MATTHEW	The Forsaken Merman	20
THE BIBLE	David's Lament for Jonathan	132
BINYON, LAURENCE	The Little Dancers	66
BLAKE, WILLIAM	The Tiger	88
	Piping down the Valleys Wild	15
BRIDGES, ROBERT	London Snow	77
BROWNING, ROBERT	Boot and Saddle	135
	Hervé Riel	89
	Home Thoughts from the Sea	138
	Incident of the French Camp	133
BURNS, ROBERT	For A' That, and A' That	43
	Macpherson's Farewell	124
	Mary Morison	107
	Open the Door to Me, Oh!	104
BYRON, GEORGE GORDON, LORD	The Shipwreck	61
	The Vision of Belshazzar	130
COLERIDGE, SAMUEL TAYLOR	*From* Frost at Midnight	80
COLLINS, WILLIAM	How Sleep the Brave	141
DE LA MARE, WALTER	Silver	114
	The Listeners	16
FLECKER, JAMES ELROY	The Golden Journey to Samarkand	159
GIBSON, WILFRID WILSON	The Parrots	81
HARVEY, FREDERICK WILLIAM	Ducks	83
HOGG, JAMES	Bonnie Prince Charlie	137
	Kilmeny	26
	The Skylark	86
KEATS, JOHN	La Belle Dame sans Merci	34
	Pictures from I Stood Tiptoe upon a Little Hill	52
LONGFELLOW, HENRY WADSWORTH	My Lost Youth	153
LOVELACE, RICHARD	To Althea from Prison	105
MACDONALD, GEORGE	The Yerl o' Waterydeck	97
MALORY, SIR THOMAS	Le Morte D'Arthur	38

		Page
MASEFIELD, JOHN	A Ballad of Cape St. Vincent	139
	The Golden City of St. Mary	152
MONRO, HAROLD	Overheard on a Saltmarsh	18
MORDAUNT, THOMAS	Sound, Sound the Clarion	96
MUIR, A.	The Stranger	42
MURRAY, GEORGE GILBERT	*From* A Chorus of Euripides	74
NAIRNE, CAROLINA, LADY	Will Ye No Come Back Again?	136
NEWBOLT, SIR HENRY	San Stefano	11
NOYES, ALFRED	The Highwayman	108
OGILVIE, WILL	The Raiders	118
O'SULLIVAN, SEUMAS	A Piper	65
PEACOCK, THOMAS LOVE	The War Song of Dinas Vawr	122
RALEIGH, SIR WALTER	The Fight about the Isles of Açores	149
SCOTT, SIR WALTER	Harlaw	128
	Lucy Ashton's Song	96
	Pibroch of Donuil Dhu	126
	Sir William of Deloraine	120
	The Foray	121
SHAKESPEARE, WILLIAM	Autolycus' Songs	41
	Caliban's Speech	156
	Clarence's Speech	157
	From As You Like It	47
	From The Merchant of Venice	73
	From The Tempest 103 *and*	154
	Oberon's Speech	156
	Orpheus	72
	When Icicles Hang by the Wall	79
SQUIRE, SIR JOHN	The Ship	163
STEVENSON, ROBERT LOUIS	A Camp	46
	I Will Make You Brooches	51
	The Contest in Music	67
	The Vagabond	45
TENNYSON, ALFRED, LORD	Morte D'Arthur	36
	The Revenge	142
	The Splendour Falls on Castle Walls	14
THOMAS, EDWARD	Two Pewits	82
WEBSTER, JOHN	Call for the Robin Redbreast and the Wren	158
WORDSWORTH, WILLIAM	Reverie of Poor Susan	75
	The Ascent of Snowdon	116
	To a Skylark	87
	Westminster Bridge	76

MEMORANDA

OR

THINGS DESERVING TO BE REMEMBERED

1. "Poesy only instructs as it delights."

    First of all, then, you must enjoy the poem. You cannot know it unless you enjoy it.

2. One of the most delightful things in poetry is its rhythm. The two lines,

    (1) *The splèndour fálls on cástle wálls,*

    (2) *And ìnto the mídnight we gálloped abréast,*

    have each four beats, or stressed syllables. Yet their rhythms are quite different, because the one has many more unstressed syllables than the other. The movement of the first is slow and dignified, while the second gallops.

3. Most of the poems in this book are in rhyme. Where it interests you, you will hear it more clearly if you draw up a rhyme scheme. Thus call the first line a; if the second rhymes with it, call it also a; if not, call it b; and so on. The rhyme scheme of the first stanza of the first poem in this book is *a b a b c d c d*.

4. The language of poetry is, of all language, the most delightful in sound, the richest in meaning.

5. Poetry must be read aloud, or you lose its music, the music of its rhythm, its rhyme, its language.

OFF THE GROUND

SAN STEFANO
(A Ballad of the Bold *Menelaus*)

It was morning at St. Helen's, in the great and gallant days,
    And the sea beneath the sun glittered wide,
When the frigate set her courses, all a-shimmer in the haze,
    And she hauled her cable home and took the tide.
She'd a right fighting company, three hundred men and more,   5
    Nine and forty guns in tackle running free;
And they cheered her from the shore for her colours at the fore,
    When the bold *Menelaus* put to sea.

She'd a right fighting company, three hundred men and more,
    Nine and forty guns in tackle running free;   10
And they cheered her from the shore for her colours at the fore,
    When the bold Menelaus *put to sea.*

She was clear of Monte Cristo, she was heading for the land,
    When she spied a pennant red and white and blue;
They were foemen, and they knew it, and they'd half a league in hand,   15
    But she flung aloft her royals and she flew.
She was nearer, nearer, nearer, they were caught beyond a doubt,
    But they slipped her, into Orbetello Bay,
And the lubbers gave a shout as they paid their cables out,
    With the guns grinning round them where they lay.   20

Now Sir Peter was a captain of a famous fighting race,
   Son and grandson of an admiral was he;
And he looked upon the batteries, he looked upon the chase,
   And he heard the shout that echoed out to sea.
And he called across the decks, "Ay! the cheering might be late   25
   If they kept it till the *Menelaus* runs;
Bid the master and his mate heave the lead and lay her straight
   For the prize lying yonder by the guns."

When the summer moon was setting, into Orbetello Bay
   Came the *Menelaus* gliding like a ghost;   30
And her boats were manned in silence, and in silence pulled away,
   And in silence every gunner took his post.
With a volley from her broadside the citadel she woke,
   And they hammered back like heroes all the night;
But before the morning broke she had vanished through the smoke   35
   With her prize upon her quarter grappled tight.

It was evening at St. Helen's, in the great and gallant time,
   And the sky behind the down was flushing far;
And the flags were all a-flutter, and the bells were all a-chime,
   When the frigate cast her anchor off the bar.   40
She'd a right fighting company, three hundred men and more,
   Nine and forty guns in tackle running free;
And they cheered her from the shore for her colours at the fore,
   When the bold *Menelaus* came from sea.

*She'd a right fighting company, three hundred men and more, 45
  Nine and forty guns in tackle running free;
And they cheered her from the shore for her colours at the fore,
  When the bold* Menelaus *came from sea.*

Sir HENRY NEWBOLT
(20th Century)

The captain was Sir Peter Parker, son of Admiral Christopher Parker, and grandson of Admiral Sir Peter Parker, the friend of Nelson. He fell in action in 1814.

San Stefano, on Orbetello Bay, was the scene of the fight. It is situated on the coast of Italy, due east of the island of Monte Cristo.

1. Compare line 1 of this poem with the two lines given on page 10. What does the rhythm here suggest?

2. What is the rhyme scheme of the first stanza?

3. Here is stanza 2 turned into prose:

    " The *Menelaus* had just left Monte Cristo astern and was heading for the mainland, when the look-out man spied a ship ahead flying the red, white, and blue pennant. This was an enemy ship and she had a lead of about a mile and a half, but Sir Peter ordered us to set every stitch she could carry and give chase. We overhauled her, hand-over-fist, and thought we had caught her, when she slipped into Orbetello Bay, ran in under the guns of the batteries, and dropped her anchor, while her crew cheered at their escape."

    What are the main differences between this and the poetry?

4. Lines 29-32. Note the effect of ghostly silence produced. What need is there for this if they are going to awake the citadel with a volley (line 33)?

5. This poem is a series of pictures. How many? Give a name to each.

Notes: page 165.

THE SPLENDOUR FALLS ON CASTLE WALLS

The splendour falls on castle walls
  And snowy summits old in story:
The long light shakes across the lakes,
  And the wild cataract leaps in glory.
Blow, bugle, blow, set the wild echoes flying,   5
Blow, bugle; answer, echoes, dying, dying, dying.

O hark, O hear! how thin and clear,
  And thinner, clearer, farther going!
O sweet and far from cliff and scar
  The horns of Elfland faintly blowing!   10
Blow, let us hear the purple glens replying:
Blow, bugle; answer, echoes, dying, dying, dying.

O love, they die in yon rich sky,
  They faint on hill or field or river:
Our echoes roll from soul to soul,   15
  And grow for ever and for ever.
Blow, bugle, blow, set the wild echoes flying,
And answer, echoes, answer, dying, dying, dying.

TENNYSON
(1809-1892)

1. This poem is famous for the beauty of its sound. Note in the first stanza:
    (a) the rhythm (see page 10);
    (b) the beautiful scheme of rhyme, perfectly repeated in the other stanzas;
    (c) the alliteration in lines 2 and 3;
    (d) the liquid sound due to the frequent recurrence of the letter *l*.
2. Line 10. What are the horns of Elfland?
3. How do the echoes of stanzas 1 and 2 differ from "Our echoes" in line 15?

Notes: page 165.

PIPING DOWN THE VALLEYS WILD

Piping down the valleys wild,
   Piping songs of pleasant glee,
On a cloud I saw a child,
   And he laughing said to me:

" Pipe a song about a Lamb!"   5
   So I piped with merry cheer.
" Piper, pipe that song again;"
   So I piped: he wept to hear.

" Drop thy pipe, thy happy pipe;
   Sing thy songs of happy cheer!"   10
So I sang the same again,
   While he wept with joy to hear.

" Piper, sit thee down and write
   In a book that all may read."
So he vanished from my sight;   15
   And I plucked a hollow reed,

And I made a rural pen,
   And I stained the water clear,
And I wrote my happy songs
   Every child may joy to hear.   20

               BLAKE
            (1757-1827)

1. There were four beats in the line in the last poem, and there are four in this. Why is the rhythm so different?
2. How many of the stanzas have the same scheme of rhyme as the first?
3. This is the introduction to a volume of poems for children, one being his " Song about a Lamb." Point out anything that makes this poem suitable for its purpose.
4. How does stanza 4 differ from stanza 3?
5. What effect has the repitition of " And " upon the meaning and the reading of stanzas 4 and 5?

Notes: page 166.

THE LISTENERS

" Is there anybody there ? " said the Traveller,
  Knocking on the moonlit door ;
And his horse in the silence champed the grasses
  Of the forest's ferny floor :
And a bird flew up out of the turret,
  Above the Traveller's head :
And he smote upon the door again a second time ;
  " Is there anybody there ? " he said.
But no one descended to the Traveller ;
  No head from the leaf-fringed sill
Leaned over and looked into his grey eyes,
  Where he stood perplexed and still.
But only a host of phantom listeners
  That dwelt in the lone house then
Stood listening in the quiet of the moonlight
  To that voice from the world of men :
Stood thronging the faint moonbeams on the dark stair,
  That goes down to the empty hall,
Hearkening in an air stirred and shaken
  By the lonely Traveller's call.
And he felt in his heart their strangeness,
  Their stillness answering his cry,
While his horse moved, cropping the dark turf
  'Neath the starred and leafy sky ;
For he suddenly smote on the door, even
  Louder, and lifted his head :
" Tell them I came, and no one answered,
  That I kept my word," he said.
Never the least stir made the listeners,
  Though every word he spake
Fell echoing through the shadowiness of the still house
  From the one man left awake :

Ay, they heard his foot upon the stirrup,
   And the sound of iron on stone,
And how the silence surged softly backward,   35
   When the plunging hoofs were gone.

WALTER DE LA MARE
(*20th Century*)

1. This poem is famous for its atmosphere (see question 10, below). It must be read aloud.

2. Draw up a rhyme scheme for lines 1-8. In which of these lines do you find alliteration?

3. Line 5. Why did the bird fly up out of the turret?

4. Line 7. Why " smote "? Would " knocked " do as well? Is there anything strange about the metre of this line? What would be the effect of omitting " again "?

5. How would you read lines 8, 15, 17-18?

6. Lines 25-28. Why does the traveller do this? To whom is he speaking?

7. How would you read lines 28, 31 and 33-36?

8. Why is the picture so indefinite?

9. What has the poet not told us that we should like to know? Why did he not tell us?

10. Have you discovered what is meant by the atmosphere of a poem, and why you have been asked so often how you would read such and such a line?

   Notes: page 166.

OVERHEARD ON A SALTMARSH

Nymph, nymph, what are your beads?
Green glass, goblin. Why do you stare at them?
Give them me.
      No.
Give them me. Give them me.
          No.
Then I will howl all night in the reeds,
Lie in the mud and howl for them.
Goblin, why do you love them so?
They are better than stars or water,
Better than voices of winds that sing,
Better than any man's fair daughter,
Your green glass beads on a silver ring.
Hush, I stole them out of the moon.
Give me your beads, I want them.
         No.
I will howl in a deep lagoon
For your green glass beads, I love them so.
Give them me. Give them.
         No.

HAROLD MONRO
(*20th Century*)

1. The poem consists of a conversation between the Goblin and the Nymph. Pick out all the Goblin's speeches.

2. Why is there no description of the Goblin and the Nymph?

3. If two pupils are to read this poem aloud to the class where should they be placed?

4. How is the Nymph treating the Goblin?

5. How would you read the Goblin's speeches?

6. What is the most difficult word to read in the poem?

Notes: page 168.

TREASURE-TROVE

Do you mind rinnin' barefit
In the saft, summer mist,
Liltin' and linkin' on the steep hill-heids?
In below your tartan shawl, your hand wad aye twist
Your bonnie green beads.   5

Do you mind traivellin', traivellin'
Ower and ower the braes,
Reistlin' the heather, and keekin' 'naith the weeds,
Seekin' and greetin' in the cauld weet days
For your tint green beads?   10

Whist! Dinna rouse him,
The auld sleepin' man—
Steek the door; the mune-licht's on the lone hill-heids—
Wee elfin craturs is delvin' in the san',
They canna miss the glimmer   15
O' your auld green beads.

Here they come, the wee folk,
Speedin' fast and fleet—
There's a queer, low lauchin' on the grey hill-heids—
And the bricht drops, glancin', followin' at their feet—   20
It's green, green beads—
The last ye 'll ever see o' your bonnie green beads.
                                            MARION ANGUS
                                            (20th Century)

barefit : *barefooted*
reistlin' : *rustling, beating*
keekin' : *peering*
greetin' : *crying*
tint : *lost*
steek : *close*
lauchin' : *laughing*

1. This poem has a delightful rhythm. How many beats are there in each line of the first stanza?
2. In this poem and the last the beads are green. Why?
3. Which is the most eerie stanza and which the most eerie line?
4. Compare this poem with the last. In which do you feel the eerie atmosphere more, in which are the spirits more alive, and which do you prefer?

   Notes: page 168.

THE FORSAKEN MERMAN

Come, dear children, let us away
Down and away below!
Now my brothers call from the bay.
Now the great winds shoreward blow,
Now the salt tides seaward flow, 5
Now the wild white horses play,
Champ and chafe and toss in the spray.
Children dear, let us away!
This way, this way!

Call her once before you go— 10
Call once yet!
In a voice that she will know:
"Margaret! Margaret!"
Children's voices should be dear
(Call once more) to a mother's ear; 15
Children's voices, wild with pain—
Surely she will come again!
Call her once and come away;
This way, this way!
"Mother dear, we cannot stay! 20
The wild white horses foam and fret."
Margaret! Margaret!

Come, dear children, come away down
Call no more!

One last look at the white-wall'd town,   25
And the little grey church on the windy shore,
Then come down!
She will not come though you call all day;
Come away, come away!

Children dear, was it yesterday   30
We heard the sweet bells over the bay?
In the caverns where we lay,
Through the surf and through the swell,
The far-off sound of a silver bell?
Sand-strewn caverns, cool and deep,   35
Where the winds are all asleep;
Where the spent lights quiver and gleam,
Where the salt weed sways in the stream,
Where the sea-beasts, ranged all round,
Feed in the ooze of their pasture-ground;   40
Where the sea-snakes coil and twine,
Dry their mail and bask in the brine;
Where great whales come sailing by,
Sail and sail, with unshut eye,
Round the world for ever and aye?   45
When did music come this way?
Children dear, was it yesterday?

Children dear, was it yesterday
(Call yet once) that she went away?
Once she sate with you and me,   50
On a red gold throne in the heart of the sea,
And the youngest sate on her knee.
She comb'd its bright hair, and she tended it well,
When down swung the sound of a far-off bell.

She sigh'd, she look'd up through the clear green sea; 55
She said: " I must go, for my kinsfolk pray
In the little grey church on the shore to-day.
'Twill be Easter-time in the world—ah me!
And I lose my poor soul, Merman! here with thee."
I said: " Go up, dear heart, through the waves; 60
Say thy prayer, and come back to the kind sea-caves!"
She smiled, she went up through the surf in the bay.
Children dear, was it yesterday?

Children dear, were we long alone?
" The sea grows stormy, the little ones moan; 65
Long prayers," I said, " in the world they say;
Come!" I said; and we rose through the surf in the bay.
We went up the beach, by the sandy down
Where the sea-stocks bloom, to the white-wall'd town;
Through the narrow paved streets, where all was still, 70
To the little grey church on the windy hill.
From the church came a murmur of folk at their prayers,
But we stood without in the cold blowing airs.
We climb'd on the graves, on the stones worn with rains,
And we gazed up the aisle through the small leaded panes. 75
She sate by the pillar; we saw her clear:
" Margaret, hist! come quick, we are here!

Dear heart," I said, " we are long alone;
The sea grows stormy, the little ones moan."
But, ah, she gave me never a look, 80
For her eyes were seal'd to the holy book!
Loud prays the priest; shut stands the door.
Come away, children, call no more!
Come away, come down, call no more

Down, down, down! 85
Down to the depths of the sea!
She sits at her wheel in the humming town,
Singing most joyfully.
Hark what she sings   " O joy, O joy,
For the humming street, and the child with its toy! 90
For the priest, and the bell, and the holy well;
For the wheel where I spun,
And the blessed light of the sun!"
And so she sings her fill,
Singing most joyfully, 95
Till the spindle drops from her hand,
And the whizzing wheel stands still.
She steals to the window, and looks at the sand,
And over the sand at the sea;
And her eyes are set in a stare; 100
And anon there breaks a sigh,
And anon there drops a tear,
From a sorrow-clouded eye,
And a heart sorrow-laden,
A long, long sigh; 105
For the cold strange eyes of a little Mermaiden
And the gleam of her golden hair.

Come away, away children;
Come children, come down!
The hoarse wind blows coldly;   110
Lights shine in the town.
She will start from her slumber
When gusts shake the door;
She will hear the winds howling,
Will hear the waves roar.   115
We shall see, while above us
The waves roar and whirl,
A ceiling of amber,
A pavement of pearl.
Singing: "Here came a mortal,   120
But faithless was she!
And alone dwell for ever
The kings of the sea."

But, children, at midnight,
When soft the winds blow,   125
When clear falls the moonlight,
When spring-tides are low;
When sweet airs come seaward
From heaths starr'd with broom,
And high rocks throw mildly   130
On the blanch'd sands a gloom;
Up the still, glistening beaches,
Up the creeks we will hie,
Over banks of bright seaweed
The ebb-tide leaves dry.   135
We will gaze, from the sand-hills,
At the white, sleeping town;

At the church on the hill-side—
And then come back down;
Singing: "There dwells a loved one,   140
But cruel is she!
She left lonely for ever
The kings of the sea."

ARNOLD
(1822-1888)

1. Can you tell from the first stanza whether this poem will be sad or gay?

2. Lines 3, 4, 5, 6 all begin with "now". If we change "now" to "and" in 4, 5, 6, what do we lose? Try the same with "where" in lines 36-43, and "when" in lines 125-128.

3. The rhythm and rhyme schemes here are very interesting. How do you read lines 1-22? Draw up the rhyme scheme.

4. We might say that the real story begins in stanza 5 (line 48). What is the poet doing in the first four stanzas?

5. Which stanza gives you the most beautiful picture of the sea, and which the most beautiful of the shore?

6. Which do you pity more, Margaret or the Merman?

7. Compare this poem with "The Neckan" in Book II.

Notes: page 168.

KILMENY

Bonnie Kilmeny gaed up the glen;
But it wasna to meet Duneira's men,
Nor the rosy monk of the isle to see,
For Kilmeny was pure as pure could be.
It was only to hear the yorlin sing,   5
And pu' the cress-flower round the spring;
The scarlet hypp and the hindberrye,
And the nut that hung frae the hazel tree;
For Kilmeny was pure as pure could be.
But lang may her minny look o'er the wa', 10
And lang may she seek i' the green-wood shaw;
Lang the laird o' Duneira blame,
And lang, lang greet or Kilmeny come hame!

When many a day had come and fled,
When grief grew calm, and hope was dead, 15
When mess for Kilmeny's soul had been sung,
When the bedesman had pray'd and the dead-bell
 rung,
Late, late in the gloamin', when all was still,
When the fringe was red on the westlin hill,
The wood was sere, the moon i' the wane, 20
The reek o' the cot hung over the plain,
Like a little wee cloud in the world its lane;
When the ingle low'd wi' an eiry leme,
Late, late in the gloamin' Kilmeny came hame!

"Kilmeny, Kilmeny, where have you been? 25
Lang hae we sought baith holt and dean;
By linn, by ford, and green-wood tree,
Yet you are halesome and fair to see.
Where gat you that joup o' the lily scheen?
That bonnie snood of the birk sae green? 30
And these roses, the fairest that ever were seen?
Kilmeny, Kilmeny, where have you been?"

Kilmeny looked up with a lovely grace,
But nae smile was seen on Kilmeny's face;
As still was her look, and as still was her e'e, 35
As the stillness that lay on the emerant lea,
Or the mist that sleeps on a waveless sea.
For Kilmeny had been, she ken'd not where,
And Kilmeny had seen what she could not declare;
Kilmeny had been where the cock never crew, 40
Where the rain never fell, and the wind never blew.
But it seemed as the harp of the sky had rung,
And the airs of heaven played round her tongue,
When she spake of the lovely forms she had seen,
And a land where sin had never been; 45
A land of love and a land of light,
Withouten sun, or moon, or night;
Where the river swa'd a living stream,
And the light a pure celestial beam;
The land of vision, it would seem, 50
A still, an everlasting dream.

*   *   *

When a month and a day had come and gane,
Kilmeny sought the green-wood wene;
There laid her down on the leaves sae green,
And Kilmeny on earth was never mair seen. 55
But oh, the words that fell from her mouth
Were words of wonder, and words of truth!

But all the land were in fear and dread,
For they kendna whether she was living or dead.
It wasna her hame, and she couldna remain ;   60
She left this world of sorrow and pain,
And returned to the land of thought again.

Hogg
(1770-1835)

yorlin : *yellow-hammer*
hindberrye : *raspberry*
minny : *mother*
shaw : *thicket*
ingle : *hearth*
leme : *light*

joup : *mantle*
scheen : *bright*
snood : *fillet, band*
birk : *birch*
swa'd : *swelled*
wene : *home*

1. The disappearance of Kilmeny in the first stanza is strange, but her return is mysterious. How does the poet make you feel this ?

2. The second stanza forms one sentence, the last line being the principal clause. What would be the effect of putting this line first in the stanza ?

3. Note the repetition of " when " in stanza 2. See " The Forsaken Merman ", note 2, (page 168).

4. The first and last lines of the third stanza are the same. Would you read them in the same manner ?

5. Where have you heard of the birk before ?

6. Do lines 42-51 contradict lines 38-39 ?

7. Where had Kilmeny been ?

8. Lines 52-55. See note to " Thomas the Rhymer " (page 32.)

Notes : page 169.

THOMAS THE RHYMER

Thomas the Rhymer, or True Thomas, was a real person, Thomas of Ercildoune or Earlston, a village not far distant from Melrose. He lived in the 13th century, and was famous as a seer. The remains of his old tower are still to be seen in Earlston, and cut into a stone of the church at Earlston are the words:

Auld Rymer's race
Lyes in this place.

True Thomas lay on Huntlie bank;
  A ferlie he spied wi' his e'e;
And there he saw a ladye bright
  Come riding down by the Eildon tree.

Her skirt was o' the grass-green silk, 5
  Her mantle o' the velvet fyne;
At ilka tett of her horse's mane
  Hung fifty siller bells and nine.

True Thomas he pu'd aff his cap,
  And louted low down on his knee: 10
" All hail, thou mighty Queen of Heaven!
  For thy peer on earth I never did see."

" O no, O no, Thomas," she said,
  " That name does not belang to me;
I am but the Queen of fair Elfland, 15
  That am hither come to visit thee.

"Harp and carp, Thomas," she said,
  "Harp and carp along wi' me;
And if ye dare to kiss my lips,
  Sure of your bodie I will be."   20

"Betide me weal, betide me woe,
  That weird shall never daunten me."
Syne he has kiss'd her rosy lips
  All underneath the Eildon tree.

"Now ye maun go wi' me," she said,   25
  "True Thomas, ye maun go wi' me;
And ye maun serve me seven years,
  Thro' weal or woe as may chance to be."

She's mounted on her milk-white steed;
  She's ta'en True Thomas up behind: 30
And aye, whene'er her bridle rang,
  The steed gaed swifter than the wind.

O they rade on, and farther on;
  The steed gaed swifter than the wind;
Until they reach'd a desert wide,   35
  And living land was left behind.

"Light down, light down now, True Thomas,
  And lean your head upon my knee;
Abide ye there a little space,
  And I will show you ferlies three.   40

"O see ye not yon narrow road,
  So thick beset with thorns and briers?
That is the Path of Righteousness,
  Though after it but few inquires.

"And see ye not yon braid braid road, 45
    That lies across that lily leven?
That is the Path of Wickedness,
    Though some call it the Road to Heaven.

"And see ye not yon bonnie road,
    That winds about the fernie brae? 50
That is the road to fair Elfland,
    Where thou and I this night maun gae.

"But, Thomas, ye maun haud your tongue,
    Whatever ye may hear or see;
For, if ye speak word in Elfyn land, 55
    Ye'll ne'er win back to your ain countrie."

Oh they rade on, and farther on,
    And they waded through rivers aboon the knee,
And they saw neither sun nor moon,
    But they heard the roaring of the sea. 60

It was mirk, mirk night, and there was nae stern light,
    And they waded through red blude to the knee;
For a' the blude that's shed on earth
    Rins through the springs o' that countrie.

Syne they came to a garden green, 65
    And she pu'd an apple frae a tree:
"Take this for thy wages, True Thomas;
    It will give thee the tongue that can never lie."

"My tongue is mine ain," True Thomas said;
    "A gudely gift ye wad gie to me! 70
I neither dought to buy nor sell,
    At fair or tryst where I may be.

"I dought neither speak to prince or peer,
  Nor ask of grace from fair ladye."
"Now haud thy peace, Thomas," she said, 75
  "For as I say, so must it be."

He has gotten a coat of the even cloth,
  And a pair of shoon of the velvet green;
And till seven years were gane and past
  True Thomas on earth was never seen. 80

ANONYMOUS

    ferlie : *marvel*   leven : *lea*
    tett : *lock*   stern : *star*
    louted : *bowed*   dought : *could*
    carp : *speak*, or *sing*

When you visit Melrose and see the district round about, those strange looking hills, the Eildons, and the Rhymer's Glen, where

> *True Thomas lay on Huntlie bank,*

and where flourished the Eildon Tree, you feel that the whole story is true. Here is another story about True Thomas. Some years after he had returned from "Fair Elfland" while making merry with his friends, in the tower of Ercildoune, a person came running in, and told, with marks of fear and astonishment, that a hart and hind had left the neighbouring forest and were composedly and slowly parading the street of the village. When this was told to True Thomas,

> *First he woxe pale, and then woxe red,*
> *Never a word he spake but three—*
> *"My sand is run, my thread is spun,*
> *This sign regardeth me."*

The prophet instantly arose, left his habitation, and followed the wonderful animals to the forest, whence he was never seen to return.

1. Why is he called True Thomas?

2. How does the description of the Queen of Elfland (stanzas 1 and 2) differ from that of La Belle Dame (stanza 4)?

3. Stanza 5. Contrast this with "La Belle Dame sans Merci", stanzas 5, 6, 7.

4. Stanzas 11 and 12. Where have you heard of these roads before?

5. Stanzas 15 and 16 (lines 57-64) are generally thought to be among the finest in the poem. What others would you put beside them?

6. Stanza 17 (lines 65-68). This was believed to be the Garden of Eden, and the apple was pulled from the Tree of Knowledge. (See question 1, above.)

7. Read carefully stanzas 3, 6, 18, 19. What kind of man was Thomas the Rhymer?

8. In how many of the stanzas do you find dialogue or direct speech used?

Notes: page 170.

I give on the following pages "La Belle Dame sans Merci" for convenience of comparison with "Thomas the Rhymer." For questions and notes on this poem see Book II.

"Thomas the Rhymer" is one of the most famous of the old ballads. Keats' poem is one of the most famous of the new.

LA BELLE DAME SANS MERCI

" O what can ail thee, knight-at-arms,
   Alone and palely loitering ?
The sedge has wither'd from the lake,
   And no birds sing.

" O what can ail thee, knight-at-arms,
   So haggard and so woe-begone ?
The squirrel's granary is full,
   And the harvest's done.

" I see a lily on thy brow
   With anguish moist and fever dew,
And on thy cheeks a fading rose
   Fast withereth too."

" I met a lady in the meads,
   Full beautiful—a faery's child,
Her hair was long, her foot was light,
   And her eyes were wild.

" I made a garland for her head,
   And bracelets too, and fragrant zone
She look'd at me as she did love,
   And made sweet moan.

" I set her on my pacing steed
   And nothing else saw all day long,
For sidelong would she bend, and sing
   A faery's song.

"She found me roots of relish sweet,
  And honey wild and manna dew,
And sure in language strange she said
  'I love thee true.'

"She took me to her elfin grot,
  And there she wept and sigh'd full sore,
And there I shut her wild wild eyes
  With kisses four.

"And there she lulled me asleep,
  And there I dream'd—Ah! woe betide!
The latest dream I ever dream'd
  On the cold hill's side.

"I saw pale kings and princes too,
  Pale warriors, death-pale were they all:
They cried—'La belle Dame sans Merci
  Hath thee in thrall!'

"I saw their starved lips in the gloam
  With horrid warning gaped wide,
And I awoke and found me here,
  On the cold hill's side.

"And this is why I sojourn here,
  Alone and palely loitering,
Though the sedge is wither'd from the lake
  And no birds sing."

KEATS
(1795-1821)

MORTE D'ARTHUR

So all day long the noise of battle roll'd
Among the mountains by the winter sea;
Until King Arthur's table, man by man,
Had fallen in Lyonnesse about their Lord,
King Arthur: then, because his wound was deep, 5
The bold Sir Bedivere uplifted him,
Sir Bedivere, the last of all his knights,
And bore him to a chapel nigh the field,
A broken chancel with a broken cross,
That stood on a dark strait of barren land. 10
On one side lay the ocean, and on one
Lay a great water, and the moon was full.
Then spake King Arthur to Sir Bedivere:

*   *   *

"I am so deeply smitten thro' the helm
That without help I cannot last till morn. 15
Thou therefore take my brand Excalibur,
Which was my pride: for thou rememberest how
In those old days, one summer noon, an arm
Rose up from out the bosom of the lake,
Clothed in white samite, mystic, wonderful, 20
Holding the sword—and how I row'd across
And took it, and have worn it, like a king:
And, wheresoever I am sung or told
In aftertime, this also shall be known:
But now delay not: take Excalibur, 25
And fling him far into the middle mere:
Watch what thou seest, and lightly bring me word."
To him replied the bold Sir Bedivere:
"It is not meet, Sir King, to leave thee thus,
Aidless, alone, and smitten thro' the helm. 30

A little thing may harm a wounded man.
Yet I thy hest will all perform at full,
Watch what I see, and lightly bring thee word."
So saying, from the ruin'd shrine he stept
And in the moon athwart the place of tombs,   35
Where lay the mighty bones of ancient men,
Old knights, and over them the sea-wind sang
Shrill, chill, with flakes of foam. He, stepping down
By zig-zag paths, and juts of pointed rock,
Came on the shining levels of the lake.   40
There drew he forth the brand Excalibur,
And o'er him, drawing it, the winter moon,
Brightening the skirts of a long cloud, ran forth
And sparkled keen with frost against the hilt;
For all the haft twinkled with diamond sparks,   45
Myriads of topaz-lights, and jacinth-work
Of subtlest jewellery. He gazed so long
That both his eyes were dazzled, as he stood,
This way and that dividing the swift mind,
In act to throw: but at the last it seem'd   50
Better to leave Excalibur conceal'd
There in the many-knotted waterflags,
That whistled stiff and dry about the marge.
So strode he back slow to the wounded King.
Then spake King Arthur to Sir Bedivere: 55
" Hast thou perform'd my mission which I gave?
What is it thou hast seen? or what hast heard?"
And answer made the bold Sir Bedivere:
" I heard the ripple washing in the reeds,
And the wild water lapping on the crag."   60

                               TENNYSON
                               (1809-1892)

    As the poem is too long to quote in full, I give on the following pages the passage of prose from which Tennyson took the story. On page 40 you will find other fifteen lines for comparison with lines 35-43 of the prose.

LE MORTE D'ARTHUR

Therefore, said Arthur unto Sir Bedivere, take thou Excalibur, my good sword, and go with it to yonder water side, and when thou comest there I charge thee throw my sword in that water, and come again and tell me what thou there seest. My lord, said Bedivere, your commandment shall be done, and lightly bring you word again. So Sir Bedivere departed, and by the way he beheld that noble sword, that the pommel and the haft was all of precious stones; and then he said to himself: If I throw this rich sword in the water, thereof shall never come good, but harm and loss. And then Sir Bedivere hid Excalibur under a tree. And so, as soon as he might, he came again unto the king, and said he had been at the water, and had thrown the sword in the water. What saw thou there? said the king. Sir, he said, I saw nothing but waves and winds.

That is untruly said of thee, said the king, therefore go thou lightly again, and do my commandment; as thou art to me lief and dear, spare not, but throw it in. Then Sir Bedivere returned again, and took the sword in his hand; and then him thought sin and shame to throw away that noble sword, and so efte he hid the sword, and returned again, and told to the king that he had been at the water, and done his commandment. What saw thou there? said the king. Sir, I saw nothing but the waters wappe and waves wanne. Ah, traitor untrue, said King Arthur, now hast thou betrayed me twice. Who would have weened that, thou that has been to me so lief and dear? and thou art named a noble knight, and would betray me for the richness of the sword. But now go again lightly, for thy long tarrying putteth me in great jeopardy of my life, for I have taken cold. And but if thou do now as I bid thee, if ever I may see thee, I shall slay thee with mine own hands; for thou wouldst for my rich sword see me dead. Then Sir Bedivere departed,

and went to the sword, and lightly took it up, and went
to the water side, and there he bound the girdle about
the hilts, and then he threw the sword as far into the
water, as he might ; and there came an arm and an
hand above the water and met it, and caught it, and so 40
shook it thrice and brandished, and then vanished away the
hand with the sword in the water. So Sir Bedivere came
again to the king and told him what he saw.

Sir THOMAS MALORY
(c. 1469)

1. Lines 1-12 (verse). Which is your favourite line here?
2. Lines 1-5 (prose) correspond to lines 16-27 (verse). What lines of the verse correspond exactly to the prose? What has Tennyson added? Is it an improvement?
3. Lines 5-6 (prose) correspond to lines 28-33 (verse). Study them as suggested in question 2.
4. Lines 6-7 (prose), "So Sir Bedivere departed", correspond to lines 34-40 (verse). Which do you prefer, the half-line of prose or the seven lines of verse? Why? Which is the most beautiful line here?
5. Lines 7-12 (prose) correspond to lines 41-53 (verse). Why is the verse here so much better than the prose?
6. Lines 12-13 (prose) correspond to line 54 (verse). Malory says, "As *soon* as he might." Tennyson says, "So strode he back *slow*." Which do you prefer?
7. Lines 13-16 (prose) correspond to lines 55-60 (verse). Which do you prefer? Why?
8. Lines 35-43 (prose) correspond to lines 61-75 (verse). Study them as suggested in question 2. Especially compare lines 71-5 (verse) and lines 39-43 (prose).
9. Compare line 75 (verse) with line 54 (verse). Can you account for the difference?
10. Have you noticed how closely the verse at times follows the prose? Give examples.
11. Compare the metre of this poem with that of the last. You will observe that there is no rhyme.

Notes: page 170.

Then quickly rose Sir Bedivere, and ran,
And, leaping down the ridges lightly, plunged
Among the bulrush beds, and clutch'd the sword,
And strongly wheel'd and threw it. The great brand
Made lightnings in the splendour of the moon, 65
And flashing round and round, and whirl'd in an arch,
Shot like a streamer of the northern morn,
Seen where the moving isles of winter shock
By night, with noises of the northern sea.
So flash'd and fell the brand Excalibur: 70
But ere he dipt the surface, rose an arm
Clothed in white samite, mystic, wonderful,
And caught him by the hilt, and brandish'd him
Three times, and drew him under in the mere.
And lightly went the other to the King. 75

TENNYSON
(1809-1892)

AUTOLYCUS' SONGS

I

When daffodils begin to peer—
 With heigh! the doxy over the dale—
Why, then comes in the sweet o' the year,
 For the red blood reigns in the winter's pale.

II

Jog on, jog on, the footpath way,
 And merrily hent the stile—a;
A merry heart goes all the day
 Your sad tires in a mile—a.

SHAKESPEARE
(1564-1616)

1. What is the spirit of Autolycus' Songs?

 Notes: page 171.

THE STRANGER

A body cam' to oor toon,
  To oor toon cam' he,
Wi' tattered coat an' broken shoon,
  But laughter in his e'e.

Quoth he, "Ye a' are unco thrang,   5
  But unco thrang for nocht,
An' I wadna gie a lav'rock's sang,
  For a' the gear ye've bocht.

"So busy coontin' ower your gains,
  Ye never leev' at a',   10
Ye're fettered fast in gowden chains
  That eat the he'rt awa'.

"This nicht to feather beds ye'll creep,
  But never rest like me,
For I will sleep the sounder sleep,   15
  Because my he'rt is free."

An' the body gaed frae oor toon,
  An' blithely he did sing,
Wi' tattered coat an' broken shoon,
  But walkin' like a king.   20

A. MUIR
(20th Century)

body : *person*	unco : *unusually*	gear : *property*
toon : *town*	thrang : *busy*	bocht : *bought*
shoon : *shoes*	nocht : *nothing*	leev' : *live*
e'e : *eye*	lav'rock : *lark*	gaed : *went*

1. Lines 1-4. Might he be Autolycus?
2. Lines 17-20. Might he be Autolycus here?
3. Which of these two stanzas (1 or 5) gives the spirit of the poem?
4. When you finish reading the poem do you think of him walking like a king, with "laughter in his e'e"?
5. Is the last line a real conclusion?

Notes: page 171.

FOR A' THAT, AND A' THAT

Is there, for honest poverty,
  That hangs his head, and a' that?
The coward slave, we pass him by,
  We dare be poor for a' that!
For a' that, and a' that, 5
  Our toils obscure, and a' that;
The rank is but the guinea stamp;
  The man's the gowd for a' that.

What tho' on hamely fare we dine,
  Wear hodden-grey, and a' that; 10
Gie fools their silks, and knaves their wine,
  A man's a man for a' that:
For a' that, and a' that,
  Their tinsel show, and a' that;
The honest man, tho' e'er sae poor, 15
  Is king o' men for a' that.

Ye see yon birkie, ca'd a lord,
  Wha struts, and stares, and a' that;
Tho' hundreds worship at his word,
  He's but a coof for a' that: 20
For a' that, and a' that,
  His riband, star, and a' that,
The man of independent mind,
  He looks and laughs at a' that.

A prince can mak' a belted knight, 25
  A marquis, duke, and a' that;
But an honest man's aboon his might,
  Guid faith he mauna fa' that!
For a' that, and a' that,
  Their dignities, and a' that, 30
The pith o' sense, and pride o' worth,
  Are higher rank than a' that.

Then let us pray that come it may,
  As come it will for a' that,
That sense and worth, o'er a' the earth,   35
  May bear the gree, and a' that.
For a' that, and a' that,
  It's coming yet, for a' that,
That man to man the world o'er,
  Shall brothers be for a' that!   40

BURNS
(1759-1796)

a' : *all*
gowd : *gold*
hodden-gray : *natural grey*
gie : *give*
birkie : *lively young fellow*

ca'd : *called*
coof : *simpleton*
mauna fa' : *must not claim*
bear the gree : *take first place*

1. Line 3. Who is the coward slave?
2. Each stanza in this poem is constructed in the same way. Can you show how?
3. Pick out the ten lines which contain most of the wisdom of this poem.
4. Is this poem as a whole constructed in the same way as each stanza?
5. How does the spirit of this poem resemble and differ from that of "The Stranger"?
6. Compare the spirit of this poem with that of Autolycus' songs.
7.   *Worth makes the man, and want of it the fellow.*

   Compare this line from Pope with lines 7-8. Which do you prefer?

8.   *Ill fares the land, to hastening ills a prey,*
   Where wealth accumulates, and men decay:
   Princes and lords may flourish, or may fade—
   A breath can make them, as a breath has made,
   But a bold peasantry, their country's pride,
   When once destroyed, can never be supplied.

   These lines are from Goldsmith's "Deserted Village". Compare lines 3-6 with lines 25-28 of the poem. Which do you prefer?

Notes: page 172.

THE VAGABOND

Give to me the life I love,
  Let the lave go by me,
Give the jolly heaven above
  And the byway nigh me.
Bed in the bush with stars to see,   5
  Bread I dip in the river—
There's the life for a man like me,
  There's the life for ever.

Let the blow fall soon or late,
  Let what will be o'er me;   10
Give the face of earth around
  And the road before me.
Wealth I seek not, hope nor love,
  Nor a friend to know me;
All I seek, the heaven above   15
  And the road below me.

Or let autumn fall on me
  Where afield I linger,
Silencing the bird on tree,
  Biting the blue finger,   20
White as meal the frosty field—
  Warm the fireside haven—
Not to autumn will I yield,
  Not to winter even!

Let the blow fall soon or late,   25
  Let what will be o'er me;
Give the face of earth around,
  And the road before me.
Wealth I ask not, hope nor love,
  Nor a friend to know me;   30
All I ask, the heaven above
  And the road below me.

R. L. STEVENSON
(1850-1894)

A CAMP

The bed was made, the room was fit,
By punctual eve the stars were lit;
The air was still, the water ran;
No need was there for maid or man,
When we put up, my ass and I,   5
At God's green caravanserai.

R. L. STEVENSON
(1850-1894)

See "A Night Among the Pines" in "Travels with a Donkey" (R. L. Stevenson).

1. Compare the spirit of "The Vagabond" with that of "For A' That".

2. Could the Stranger be the Vagabond?

3. Could Autolycus be the Vagabond?

4. Which of these three would be happiest in "A Camp"?

Notes: page 172.

From AS YOU LIKE IT

Act I, Sc. 1

Oliver—Good Monsieur Charles. what's the new news at the new court?

Charles—There's no news at the court, sir, but the old news: that is, the old Duke is banished by his younger brother the new Duke; and three or four loving lords have put themselves into voluntary exile with him, whose lands and revenues enrich the new Duke; therefore he gives them good leave to wander.

* * *

Oliver—Where will the old Duke live?

Charles—They say he is already in the forest of Arden, and a many merry men with him; and there they live like the old Robin Hood of England: they say many young gentlemen flock to him every day, and fleet the time carelessly, as they did in the golden world.

Act II, Sc. V—The Forest

Enter Amiens, Jaques, and others

Song

Under the greenwood tree
Who loves to lie with me,
And turn his merry note
Unto the sweet bird's throat,
Come hither, come hither, come hither:
  Here shall he see
  No enemy
But winter and rough weather.

Jaq.—More, more, I prithee, more.

Ami.—It will make you melancholy, Monsieur Jaques.

Jaq.—I thank it. More, I prithee, more. I can suck melancholy out of a song, as a weasel sucks eggs. More, I prithee, more.

Ami.—Well, I'll end the song. Sirs, cover the while; the Duke will drink under this tree.

All together here

> Who doth ambition shun,
> And loves to live i' the sun,
> Seeking the food he eats,
> And pleased with what he gets,
> Come hither, come hither, come hither:
> Here shall he see
> No enemy
> But winter and rough weather.

Jaq.—I'll give you a verse to this note, that I made yesterday in despite of my invention.

Ami.—And I'll sing it.

Jaq.—Thus it goes:

> If it do come to pass
> That any man turn ass,
> Leaving his wealth and ease
> A stubborn will to please,
> Ducdame, ducdame, ducdame:
> Here shall he see
> Gross fools as he,
> And if he will come to me.

Ami.—What's that "ducdame"?

Jaq.—'Tis a Greek invocation, to call fools into a circle. I'll go sleep if I can.

Ami.—And I'll go seek the Duke: his banquet is prepared.

Scene VII—The Forest

A table set out

Enter Duke, Amiens and Lords, like outlaws

Duke—Welcome; fall to . . .
Give us some music; and, good cousin, sing.

Song

Ami.—
    Blow, blow, thou winter wind,
    Thou art not so unkind
      As man's ingratitude;
    Thy tooth is not so keen,
    Because thou art not seen,
      Although thy breath be rude.

Heigh, ho! sing, heigh, ho! unto the green holly:
Most friendship is feigning, most loving mere folly:
    Then, heigh, ho! the holly!
    This life is most jolly.

Freeze, freeze, thou bitter sky,
That dost not bite so nigh
  As benefits forgot:
Though thou the waters warp,
Thy sting is not so sharp
  As friend remember'd not.

Heigh, ho! sing, heigh, ho! unto the green holly:
Most friendship is feigning, most loving mere folly:
  Then, heigh, ho! the holly!
This life is most jolly.

SHAKESPEARE
(1564-1616)

1. Is the spirit of Amiens' first song, "Under the greenwood tree", similar to that of "The Vagabond" or of Autolycus' Songs?

2. What makes this song especially appropriate?

3. What does the rhythm of the refrain recall?

4. How would you describe Jaques' song, and how would you pronounce "Ducdame"?

5. In what way does the spirit of Amiens' second song, "Blow, blow, thou winter wind", differ from that of the first?

Notes: page 173.

I WILL MAKE YOU BROOCHES

I will make you brooches and toys for your delight
Of bird-song at morning and star-shine at night.
I will make a palace fit for you and me
Of green days in forests and blue days at sea.

I will make my kitchen, and you shall keep your room, 5
Where white flows the river and bright blows the broom,
And you shall wash your linen and keep your body white
In rainfall at morning and dewfall at night.

And this shall be for music when no one else is near,
The fine song for singing, the rare song to hear! 10
That only I remember, that only you admire,
Of the broad road that stretches and the roadside fire.

R. L. STEVENSON
(1850-1894)

1. Lines 1-2. How can you make brooches and toys of bird-song and star-shine?

2. Line 4. Would it not be better and more accurate to say, " Of days in green forests and days on the blue sea "?

3. Line 6. What would be the effect of changing " white " to " clean " ?

4. The spirit of this poem recalls especially two poems among the last seven or eight. Which two?

Notes: page 174.

Pictures from

I STOOD TIPTOE UPON A LITTLE HILL

The clouds were pure and white as flocks new-shorn,
And fresh from the clear brook; sweetly they slept
On the blue fields of heaven, and then there crept
A little noiseless noise among the leaves,
Born of the very sigh that silence heaves.   5

Here are sweet peas, on tiptoe for a flight
With wings of gentle flush o'er delicate white
And taper fingers catching at all things,
To bind them all about with tiny rings.

How silent comes the water round that bend!   10
Not the minutest whisper does it send
To the o'erhanging sallows: blades of grass
Slowly across the chequer'd shadows pass.

Where swarms of minnows show their little heads,
Staying their wavy bodies 'gainst the streams,   15
To taste the luxury of sunny beams
Temper'd with coolness. How they ever wrestle
With their own sweet delight, and ever nestle
Their silver bellies on the pebbly sand!
If you but scantily hold out the hand,   20
That very instant not one will remain;
But turn your eye, and they are there again.

KEATS
(1795-1821)

1. How many of these pictures do you know?
2. Which of them appeal to the eye, which to the ear, and which to other senses?
3. Which picture do you prefer?
4. Some of the lines here everyone would want to remember. Pick them out.

Notes: page 175.

THE DOWIE DENS O' YARROW

Late at e'en, drinkin' the wine,
And ere they had paid the lawin'
They set a combat them atween
To fight it at the dawin'.

"You took our sister for your wife   5
And you ne'er made her your marrow
You stole her frae her father's hame
When she was the Rose o' Yarrow."

"I took your sister for my wife,
Made her my ain dear marrow.   10
I got her frae her father's han'
And she's aye the Rose o' Yarrow."

"O! though you be our sister's lord
We'll cross our swords the morrow."
"And though ye be guid-brithers mine   15
I'll fight wi' ye on Yarrow."

Hame to his leddy he has gane
And said, "My winsome marrow,
I've gien my word to keep a tryst
In the dowie dens o' Yarrow."   20

"O! staye at hame my ain dear lord
O! staye, my ain dear marrow.
My cruel brithers will you slay
In the dowie dens o' Yarrow."

"Hoots-toots, guid-wife, dry up your tears, 25
For what needs a' this sorrow;
For if I gang, I'll sune return
Frae the dowie dens o' Yarrow."

She kissed his cheeks, she kaimed his hair.
Her heart forbodin' sorrow, 30
But she's belted him wi' his guid brand,
And he's awa' to Yarrow.

As he gaed up the Tennies bank
I wat he gaed wi' sorrow,
For there he spied nine arméd men 35
In the dowie dens o' Yarrow.

"O! come you here to hunt or hawk
The bonnie forest thorough?
Or come you here to pairt your land
In the dowie dens o' Yarrow?" 40

"I come not here to hunt or hawk
The bonnie forest thorough,
Nor come I here to pairt my land
In the dowie dens o' Yarrow.

"If I see right I coont ye nine, 45
Ye'll ken if I coont thorough,
Yet will I stand while hauds this brand
In the dowie dens o' Yarrow.

"If ye attack me nine to ane,
Then may God sen' ye sorrow.
But yet I'll fight ye, ane to nine, 50
In the dowie dens o' Yarrow."

Four has he hurt, and five has slain
On the bluidy banks o' Yarrow,
When a coward loon cam' him behind   55
And ran his body thorough.

" Gae hame, gae hame, guid-brither John,
And tell my winsome marrow,
Tell her, oh tell her, her true love   60
Will ne'er return frae Yarrow."

Oot o'er the hills, guid-brither John
Went wi' his tale o' sorrow.
Wha should he meet but his sister dear
Fast rinnin' on to Yarrow.

" I dream't a dreary dream yestreen: 65
God keep us a' frae sorrow.
I dream't I pu'd the birk sae green
Wi' my true love on Yarrow."

" I'll read your dream, my sister dear,
I'll read it unto sorrow.   70
You pu'd the birk wi' your true love.
He's deid! He's killed! on Yarrow."

She pu'd the ribbons frae her heid
They were baith braid an' narrow,
And o'er the hills she went wi' speed   75
To the dowie dens o' Yarrow.

She's ta'en him in her airmis twa
Wi' mickle dule an' sorrow,
And kissed his wounds ilk ane an a',
The wounds he's got on Yarrow.   80

She kissed his cheeks, she kaimed his hair
As aft she had dune afore O!
And then for syne her heart did break.
And they sleep sound on Yarrow.

ANONYMOUS

dowie : *gloomy*	tryst : *appointment*
lawin' : *reckoning*	Tennies : *name of a farm*
marrow : *equal, companion*	yestreen : *last night*
	loon : *fellow*
guid-brithers : *brothers-in-law*	dule : *grief*

1. Who is speaking in lines 5-8, 9-12, 13-14, and 15-16 ?
2. Often one side is anxious for a quarrel, while the other is being forced into it. Who is making the quarrel here ?
3. Are the time and place suitable for a quarrel ?
4. What difference should there be in the manner in which you read the speeches of the two sides ?
5. What is the difference between line 8 and line 12 ?
6. How would you read lines 25-28 ?
7. Lines 29-32. Which has the heavier burden to bear ?
8. In "The Lady of the Lake", Fitz-James suddenly finds himself face to face with his enemy, Roderick Dhu, and all his men. This is how Scott puts it :

    Fitz-James was brave : Though to his heart
    The life-blood thrill'd with sudden start.
    He mann'd himself with dauntless air,
    Return'd the Chief his haughty stare,
    His back against a rock he bore,
    And firmly placed his foot before :
    " Come one, come all ! this rock shall fly
    From its firm base as soon as I."

    Compare this with lines 45-52.

9. Line 57. Who is guid-brither John ?
10. Lines 65-68. Why does she call it a dreary dream ?
11. In how many of the stanzas do you find dialogue or direct speech used ?

Notes : page 175.

SIR PATRICK SPENS

The king sits in Dunfermline toun,
  Drinking the blude-red wine;
"O whaur will I get a skeely skipper,
  To sail this ship o' mine?"

Then up and spake an eldern knight   5
  Sat at the king's right knee:
"Sir Patrick Spens is the best sailor
  That ever sail'd the sea."

The king has written a braid letter,
  And seal'd it wi' his hand,   10
And sent it to Sir Patrick Spens
  Was walking on the strand.

"To Noroway, to Noroway,
  To Noroway owre the faem;
The king's daughter o' Noroway,   15
  'Tis thou maun bring her hame."

The first word that Sir Patrick read,
  A loud laugh laughed he;
The neist word that Sir Patrick read,
  The tear blinded his e'e.   20

"O wha is this has done this deed,
  And tauld the king o' me,
To send us out at this time o' the year
  To sail upon the sea?

"Be it wind, be it weet, be it hail, be it sleet   25
  Our ship maun sail the faem;
The king's daughter o' Noroway
  'Tis we maun bring her hame."

They hoysed their sails on Monenday morn,
  Wi' a' the speed they may;
They hae landed in Noroway
  Upon a Wodensday.

        *   *   *

" Mak' ready, mak' ready, my merry men a',
  Our guid ship sails the morn."
" Now ever alack, my master dear,
  I fear a deidly storm.

' I saw the new moon late yestreen,
  Wi' the auld moon in her arm;
And if we gang to sea, master,
  I fear we'll come to harm ".

They hadna sail'd a league, a league,
  A league but barely three,
When the lift grew dark, and the wind blew loud,
  And gurly grew the sea.

The ankers brak, and the tap-mast lap,
  It was sic a deidly storm;
And the waves cam owre the broken ship,
  Till a' her sides were torn.

" O whaur will I get a guid sailor
  Will tak' the helm in hand,
Till I gang up to the tall tap-mast
  To see if I can spy land?"

" O here am I, a sailor guid,
  To tak' the helm in hand,
Till ye gang up to the tall tap-mast—
  But I fear ye'll ne'er spy land."

He hadna gane a step, a step,
   A step but barely ane,
When a bolt flew out o' the guid ship's side,
   And the saut sea it cam' in.   60

"Gae fetch a wab o' the silken claith,
   Anither o' the twine,
And wap them into our guid ship's side,
   And let na the sea come in."

They fetched a wab o' the silken claith,   65
   Anither o' the twine,
And they wapp'd them into the guid ship's side,
   But aye the sea cam' in.

O laith, laith were our guid Scots lords
   To weet their cork-heeled shoon,   70
But lang or a' the play was played,
   They wat their hats abune.

And mony was the feather-bed
   That fluttered on the faem,
And mony was the guid lord's son   75
   That never mair cam' hame.

O lang, lang may the ladies sit,
   Wi' their fans into their hand,
Before they see Sir Patrick Spens
   Come sailing to the strand.   80

And lang, lang may the maidens sit,
   Wi' the gowd kaims in their hair,
A-waiting for their ain dear loves,
   For them they'll see nae mair.

> Half owre, half owre to Aberdour,
>   It's fifty fathom deep,
> And there lies guid Sir Patrick Spens,
>   Wi' the Scots lords at his feet.

ANONYMOUS

skeely: *skilful.*
gurly: *surly, grim.*
wap: *stuff.*
or: *before.*

1. Line 1. Who is the king?

2. How many beats are there in each of the first four lines, and what is the rhyme scheme? This is the regular ballad stanza.

3. Lines 13-16. If we omitted line 13, what should we lose?

4. Lines 21-24. What time of the year was it?

5. Lines 37-38. Compare the following passage from Coleridge:

    > Well! If the Bard was weather-wise, who made
    > The grand old ballad of Sir Patrick Spence,
    > This night, so tranquil now, will not go hence
    > Unroused by winds, that ply a busier trade
    > Than those which mould yon cloud in lazy flakes...
    >
    > For lo! the New-moon winter-bright!
    > And overspread with phantom light,
    > (With swimming phantom light o'erspread
    > But rimmed and circled by a silver thread)
    > I see the old Moon in her lap, foretelling
    > The coming-on of rain and squally blast.

6. Lines 41-44. What is striking about this stanza?

7. Lines 69-84. Is the shipwreck well described? (See next poem.)

8. Which stanza in the poem do you like best?

Notes: page 176.

THE SHIPWRECK

'Twas twilight, and the sunless day went down
  Over the waste of waters; like a veil
Which, if withdrawn, would but disclose the frown
  Of one whose hate is mask'd but to assail;
Thus to their hopeless eyes the night was shown,   5
  And grimly darkled o'er their faces pale,
And the dim desolate deep: twelve days had Fear
Been their familiar, and now Death was here.

Then rose from sea to sky the wild farewell—
  Then shriek'd the timid and stood still the brave,   10
Then some leap'd overboard with dreadful yell,
  As eager to anticipate the grave;
And the sea yawn'd around her like a hell,
  And down she suck'd with her the whirling wave,
Like one who grapples with his enemy,   15
And strives to strangle him before he die.

And first one universal shriek there rush'd,
  Louder than the loud ocean, like a crash
Of echoing thunder; and then all was hush'd,
  Save the wild wind and the remorseless dash   20
Of billows; but at intervals there gush'd,
  Accompanied with a convulsive splash,
A solitary shriek, the bubbling cry
Of some strong swimmer in his agony.

      ("Don Juan", *Canto II, Stanzas* 49, 52, 53)
                                  BYRON (1788-1824)

1. Compare this with the shipwreck in "Sir Patrick Spens". Which is the more terrible? Why?
2. Is there anything in this poem that has an effect like that of the last stanza in "Sir Patrick Spens"?
3. Many of the most striking effects in stanza 3 are obtained by the use of adjectives, *e.g.*, lines 20-24—wild, remorseless, convulsive, solitary, bubbling, strong. What are the most telling words in stanzas 1 and 2?

Notes: page 177.

THE BONNIE EARL OF MURRAY

(*First Version*)

"Open the gates,
  And let him come in;
He is my brother Huntly,
  He'll do him nae harm."

The gates they were opened, 5
  They let him come in;
But fause traitor Huntly,
  He did him great harm.

He's ben, and ben,
  And ben to his bed; 10
And wi' a sharp rapier
  He's stabbed him dead.

The lady came down the stair,
  Wringing her hands;
"He has slain the Earl o' Murray, 15
  The flower o' Scotland."

But Huntly lap on his horse,
  Rade to the King.
"Ye're welcome hame, Huntly,
  And whaur hae ye been? 20

"Whaur hae ye been?
  And how hae ye sped?"
"I've killed the Earl o' Murray,
  Dead in his bed."

"Foul fa' you, Huntly! 25
  And why did you sae?
You might have ta'en the Earl o' Murray
  And saved his life tae."

"Her bread it's to bake,
  Her yill is to brew; 30
My sister's a widow,
  And sair do I rue.

"Her corn grows ripe,
  Her meadows grow green,
But in bonnie Donibristle 35
  I darena be seen."

ANONYMOUS

THE BONNIE EARL OF MURRAY

(Second Version)

Ye Highlands and ye Lawlands,
O whaur hae ye been?
They hae slain the Earl of Murray,
And hae laid him on the green.

Now wae be to thee, Huntly, 5
And wherefore did ye sae?
I bade ye bring him wi' ye,
But forbade ye him to slay.

He was a braw gallant,
And he rade at the ring; 10
And the bonnie Earl of Murray,
O he might hae been a king.

He was a braw gallant,
And he play'd at the ba';
And the bonnie Earl of Murray   15
Was the flower amang them a'.

He was a braw gallant,
And he play'd at the glove;
And the bonnie Earl of Murray,
He was the queen's luve.   20

O lang will his Lady
Look owre the Castle Downe,
Ere she see the Earl of Murray
Come sounding through the town.

ANONYMOUS

    ben : *into the inner room*
    foul fa' you : *may an evil fate befall you*
    yill : *ale*

1. Who speaks in stanzas 1, 4, 8, 9 of the first version?

2. There are 36 lines in the first version. How many of them are in direct speech?

3. First version, lines 9-10. Drop the repetition of " ben " and make one line out of two, thus : " He's ben to his bed." Do you lose anything of importance?

4. In what is the author of the first version chiefly interested?

5. In what is the author of the second version chiefly interested?

6. Would it make any real difference if stanzas 3 and 5 of the second version were transposed?

7. Compare the atmosphere of the two versions.

8. Which of the two versions seems to you the better poem?

9. Which version do you prefer?

   Notes: page 177.

A PIPER

A piper in the streets to-day
Set up, and tuned, and started to play,
And away, away, away on the tide
Of his music we started; on every side
Doors and windows were opened wide,   5
And men left down their work and came,
And women with petticoats coloured like flame,
And little bare feet that were blue with cold
Went dancing back to the age of gold,
And all the world went gay, went gay,   10
For half an hour in the street to-day.

SEUMAS O'SULLIVAN
(20th Century)

1. This poem is part of a longer poem called "In Mercer Street". This street is in Dublin. How might you have guessed it was a street in Ireland?

2. If lines 3 and 4 read "And away on the tide of his music we started", should we have lost anything of importance?

3. How would you read line 3?

4. Lines 6, 7, 8, 10 all begin with "And". Why? See "Piping down the Valleys Wild", "The Forsaken Merman", and "Kilmeny".

5. Line 9. Why is this line particularly appropriate?

6. What words would you use to describe the atmosphere of this poem?

7. Compare the rhythm of this poem with that of the next.

   Notes: page 178.

THE LITTLE DANCERS

Lonely, save for a few faint stars, the sky
Dreams; and lonely, below, the little street
Into its gloom retires, secluded and shy.
Scarcely the dumb roar enters this soft retreat;
And all is dark, save where come flooding rays   5
From a tavern window: there, to the brisk measure
Of an organ that down in an alley merrily plays,
Two children, all alone and no one by,
Holding their tattered frocks, through an airy maze
Of motion, lightly threaded with nimble feet,   10
Dance sedately: face to face they gaze,
Their eyes shining, grave with a perfect pleasure.

LAURENCE BINYON
(20th Century)

1. How far must you read in this poem before you feel the change of atmosphere from the last?

2. Lines 1-4. How is it that this description seems neither gloomy nor sad, in spite of the words "lonely" (line 1), "lonely" (line 2), "gloom" (line 3), "dumb roar" line 4?

3. Why would it be easier to picture the scene of this poem than that of the last?

4. Which words in the last two lines emphasise how different the atmosphere is from that of "A Piper"?

5. Which of these two poems gives the deeper sense of joy?

6. In these two poems is the happiness due to the music or to the dancing?

7. Which poem has the simpler rhyme scheme? Why?

8. There are five beats in each line, yet the rhythm seems at times to change. See especially lines 2, 6, 7, 8, 9, 12.

9. Does the rhythm of this poem dance?

Notes: page 179.

THE CONTEST IN MUSIC

"Kidnapped", *Ch. XXV. In Balquhidder.*

David Balfour is lying ill in the house of Duncan Maclaren in Balquhidder, and Robin Oig Macgregor has chanced to call. Just as he is leaving, David's friend, Alan Breck Stewart, comes in.)

Just in the door, he met Alan coming in; and the two drew back and looked at each other like strange dogs. They were neither of them big men, but they seemed fairly to swell out with pride. Each wore a sword, and by a movement of his haunch, thrust clear the hilt of it, so that it might be the more readily grasped and the blade drawn.

"Mr. Stewart, I am thinking," says Robin.

"Troth, Mr. Macgregor, it's not a name to be ashamed of," answered Alan.

"I did not know ye were in my country, sir," says Robin.

"It sticks in my mind that I am in the country of my friends, the Maclarens," says Alan.

"That's a kittle point," returned the other. "There may be two words to say to that. But I think I will have heard that you are a man of your sword?"

"Unless ye were born deaf, Mr. Macgregor, ye will have heard a good deal more than that," says Alan. "I am not the only man that can draw steel in Appin; and when my kinsman and captain, Ardshiel, had a talk with a gentleman of your name, not so many years back, I could never hear that the Macgregor had the best of it."

"Do ye mean my father, sir?" says Robin.

"Well, I wouldna wonder," said Alan. "The gentleman I have in my mind had the ill-taste to clap Campbell to his name."

"My father was an old man," returned Robin. "The match was unequal. You and me would make a better pair, sir."

"I was thinking that," said Alan.

I was half out of bed, and Duncan had been hanging at the elbow of these fighting cocks ready to intervene upon the least occasion. But when that word was uttered, it was a case of now or never; and Duncan, with something of a white face to be sure, thrust himself between.

"Gentlemen," said he, "I will have been thinking of a very different matter, whateffer. Here are my pipes, and here are you two gentlemen who are baith acclaimed pipers. It's an auld dispute which one of ye's the best. Here will be a braw chance to settle it."

"Why, sir," said Alan, still addressing Robin, from whom indeed he had not so much as shifted his eyes, nor yet Robin from him, "why, sir," says Alan, "I think I will have heard some sough of the sort. Have ye music, as folk say? Are ye a bit of a piper?"

"I can pipe like a Macrimmon!" cries Robin.

"And that is a very bold word," quoth Alan.

"I have made bolder words good before now," returned Robin, "and that against better adversaries."

"It is easy to try that," says Alan.

Duncan Dhu made haste to bring out the pair of pipes that was his principal possession, and to set before his guests a mutton-ham and a bottle of that drink which they call Athole-brose, and which is made of old whisky, strained honey and sweet cream, slowly beaten together in the right order and proportion. The two enemies were still on the very breach of a quarrel; but down they sat, one upon each side of the peat fire, with a mighty show of politeness. Maclaren pressed them to taste his mutton-ham and "the wife's brose," reminding them the wife was out of Athole and had a name far and wide for her skill in that confection. But Robin put aside these hospitalities as bad for the breath.

"I would have ye to remark, sir," said Alan, "that I havena broken bread for near upon ten hours, which will be worse for the breath than any brose in Scotland."

"I will take no advantages, Mr. Stewart," replied Robin. "Eat and drink; I'll follow you."

Each ate a small portion of the ham and drank a glass of the brose to Mrs. Maclaren; and then, after a great number of civilities, Robin took the pipes and played a little spring in a very ranting manner.

"Ay, ye can blow," said Alan, and taking the instrument from his rival, he first played the same spring in a manner identical with Robin's and then wandered into variations, which, as he went on, he decorated with a perfect flight of grace-notes, such as pipers love, and call the "warblers."

I had been pleased with Robin's playing; Alan's ravished me.

"That's no very bad, Mr. Stewart," said the rival, "but ye show a poor device in your warblers."

"Me!" cried Alan, the blood starting to his face. "I give ye the lie."

"Do ye own yourself beaten at the pipes, then," said Robin, "that ye seek to change them for the sword?"

"And that's very well said, Mr. Macgregor," returned Alan; "and in the meantime" (laying a strong accent on the word) "I take back the lie. I appeal to Duncan."

"Indeed, ye need appeal to naebody," said Robin. "Ye're a far better judge than any Maclaren in Balquhidder: for it's a God's truth that you're a very creditable piper for a Stewart. Hand me the pipes."

Alan did as he asked; and Robin proceeded to imitate and correct some part of Alan's variations, which it seemed that he remembered perfectly.

"Ay, ye have music," said Alan, gloomily.

"And now be the judge yourself, Mr. Stewart," said Robin; and taking up the variations from the beginning, he worked them throughout to so new a purpose, with such ingenuity and sentiment, and with so odd a fancy and so quick a knack in the grace-notes, that I was amazed to hear him.

As for Alan, his face grew dark and hot, and he sat and gnawed his fingers, like a man under some deep affront. "Enough!" he cried. "Ye can blow the pipes—make the most of that." And he made as if to rise.

But Robin only held out his hand as if to ask for silence, and struck into the slow measure of a pibroch. It was a fine piece of music in itself, and nobly played; but it seems, besides, it was a piece peculiar to the Appin Stewarts and a chief favourite with Alan. The first notes were scarce out, before there came a change in his face; when the time quickened, he seemed to grow restless in his seat; and long before that piece was at an end, the last signs of his anger died from him, and he had no thought but for the music.

"Robin Oig," he said, when it was done, "ye are a great piper. I am not fit to blow in the same kingdom with ye. Body of me! ye have mair music in your sporran than I have in my head! And though it still sticks in my mind that I could maybe show ye another of it with the cold steel, I warn ye beforehand—it'll no' be fair! It would go against my heart to haggle a man that can blow the pipes as you can!"

Thereupon that quarrel was made up; all night long the brose was going and the pipes changing hands; and the day had come pretty bright, and the three men were none the better for what they had been taking, before Robin as much as thought upon the road.

R. L. Stevenson
(1850-1894)

1. Lines 1-7. You have seen two boys behaving like this.

2. Line 31. Note the dry manner of Alan's acceptance. Who is making the quarrel here? Compare the situation with that described in " The Dowie Dens o' Yarrow ".

    Line 45. Sough: rumour.

3. Line 47. The Macrimmons were the most famous pipers in history. Note Robin's challenge and, again, Alan's quiet, dry acceptance in lines 49-51.

4. Lines 65-73. Note the fine manners of the two, and the fine spirit, especially in lines 68-69.

5. Line 74. Alan recognises he has met a piper.

6. Lines 82-92. This is the fiercest moment of the quarrel. How would you read the words, " You're a very creditable piper for a Stewart " (lines 95-96)?

7. Lines 108-112. Alan accepts his defeat, but is only the more anxious to try it out with the sword.

8. Lines 113-114. Why does Robin do this? He has already won the contest in music and his rival has acknowledged it.

9. Lines 115-122. Note Alan's reaction to the music. Milton says that music has power to chase

    *Anguish, and doubt, and fear, and sorrow, and pain
    From mortal or immortal minds.*

    It has done so here.

10. Lines 123-130. This is the triumph of music. Why is it that Alan seems greater here than Robin? Contrast this with lines 82-92.

11. Why do you think I have included this passage of prose in an anthology of poetry?

12. I have printed a song from Shakespeare on page 72, and a passage from " The Merchant of Venice " on page 73 for comparison.

    Notes: page 180.

ORPHEUS

Orpheus with his lute made trees
And the mountain tops that freeze
  Bow themselves when he did sing;
To his music plants and flowers
Ever sprang, as sun and showers   5
  There had made a lasting spring.

Everything that heard him play,
Even the billows of the sea,
  Hung their heads, and then lay by.
In sweet music is such art,   10
Killing care and grief of heart
  Fall asleep, or, hearing, die.

                        SHAKESPEARE
                        (1564-1616)

1. Lines 1-3 and 7-9. Compare these with the following in which Gray is referring to the slaughter of the Welsh Bards:

    Cold is Cadwallo's tongue,
    That hushed the stormy main;
    Brave Urien sleeps upon his craggy bed;
    Mountains, ye mourn in vain
    Modred, whose magic song
    Made huge Plinlimmon bow his cloud-topped head.

2. Lines 4-6. Explain these three lines, especially " sprang " in line 5 and " there " in line 6.

3. Lines 10-12. If you wish to make the meaning of these lines very clear, you have but to add one word to the end of line 10.

    Notes: page 181.

From THE MERCHANT OF VENICE

Act V, Sc. I

Lorenzo—

>How sweet the moonlight sleeps upon this bank!
>Here will we sit, and let the sounds of music
>Creep in our ears: soft stillness and the night
>Become the touches of sweet harmony.
>Sit, Jessica. Look how the floor of heaven
>Is thick inlaid with patines of bright gold:
>There's not the smallest orb which thou behold'st
>But in his motion like an angel sings,
>Still quiring to the young-eyed cherubins;
>Such harmony is in immortal souls;
>But whilst this muddy vesture of decay
>Doth grossly close it in, we cannot hear it.

Enter Musicians.

>Come, ho, and wake Diana with a hymn!
>With sweetest touches pierce your mistress' ear,
>And draw her home with music.

Music

Jessica—

>I am never merry when I hear sweet music.

Lorenzo—

>The reason is, your spirits are attentive:
>For do but note a wild and wanton herd,
>Or race of youthful and unhandled colts,
>Fetching mad bounds, bellowing and neighing loud,
>Which is the hot condition of their blood;
>If they but hear perchance a trumpet sound,
>Or any air of music touch their ears,

You shall perceive them make a mutual stand,
Their savage eyes turn'd to a modest gaze
By the sweet power of music: therefore the poet
Did feign that Orpheus drew trees, stones, and floods;
Since nought so stockish, hard and full of rage,
But music for the time doth change his nature.
The man that hath no music in himself,
Nor is not moved with concord of sweet sounds,
Is fit for treasons, stratagems and spoils;
The motions of his spirit are dull as night,
And his affections dark as Erebus:
Let no such man be trusted.

SHAKESPEARE
(1564-1616)

From A CHORUS OF EURIPIDES

In the elm-woods and the oaken,
    There where Orpheus harped of old,
And the trees awoke and knew him,
    And the wild things gathered to him,
As he sang amid the broken
    Glens his music manifold.

Translated by GILBERT MURRAY
(20*th* Century)

REVERIE OF POOR SUSAN

At the corner of Wood Street, when daylight appears,
Hangs a thrush that sings loud—it has sung for three
  years :
Poor Susan has passed by the spot, and has heard
In the silence of morning the song of the bird.

'Tis a note of enchantment : what ails her ? She sees 5
A mountain ascending, a vision of trees ;
Bright volumes of vapour through Lothbury glide,
And a river flows on through the vale of Cheapside.

Green pastures she views in the midst of the dale,
Down which she so often has tripped with her pail ; 10
And a single small cottage, a nest like a dove's,
The one only dwelling on earth that she loves.

She looks, and her heart is in heaven : but they fade,
The mist and the river, the hill and the shade :
The stream will not flow, and the hill will not rise, 15
And the colours have all passed away from her eyes.

                                WORDSWORTH
                                (1770-1850)

1. Have you learned from the poem what a reverie means ?

2. Wood Street is in London. Is Susan a London girl ?

3. Why " Poor " Susan ?

4. Where in the poem does Susan leave London and where does she return ?

5. What is specially appropriate in line 4 ?

Notes : page 181.

WESTMINSTER BRIDGE

Earth has not anything to show more fair:
Dull would he be of soul who could pass by
A sight so touching in its majesty:
This City now doth, like a garment, wear
The beauty of the morning: silent, bare, 5
Ships, towers, domes, theatres, and temples lie
Open unto the fields, and to the sky;
All bright and glittering in the smokeless air.
Never did sun more beautifully steep
In his first splendour, valley, rock, or hill; 10
Ne'er saw I, never felt, a calm so deep!
The river glideth at his own sweet will:
Dear God! the very houses seem asleep;
And all that mighty heart is lying still!

WORDSWORTH
(1770-1850)

The following passage describing the same scene is from Dorothy Wordsworth's Journal:—

July 30—Left London between five and six o'clock of the morning outside the Dover coach. A beautiful morning. The city, St. Paul's, with the river—a multitude of little boats, made a beautiful sight as we crossed *Westminster Bridge;* the houses not overhung by their clouds of smoke, and were hung out endlessly; yet the sun shone so brightly, with such a pure light, that there was something like the purity of one of Nature's own grand spectacles.

1. Could this poem be called " The Reverie of William Wordsworth "? (See the preceding poem.)
2. What time in the morning is it?
3. What is the meaning of line 7?
4. What is especially worthy of note in lines 1 and 11?
5. How much of this sonnet could be applied to the bridge you know?

Notes: page 181.

LONDON SNOW

(" If this poem is read softly, pausingly, without haste, the very words will seem like snowflakes themselves, floating into the mind ; and then, the beauty and the wonder ".—*W. de la Mare.*)

When men were all asleep the snow came flying,
In large white flakes falling on the city brown,
Stealthily and perpetually settling and loosely lying,
   Hushing the latest traffic of the drowsy town ;
Deadening, muffling, stifling its murmurs failing ;   5
Lazily and incessantly floating down and down :
   Silently sifting and veiling road, roof and railing ;
Hiding difference, making unevenness even,
Into angles and crevices softly drifting and sailing.
   All night it fell, and when full inches seven   10
It lay in the depth of its uncompacted lightness,
The clouds blew off from a high and frosty heaven ;
   And all woke earlier for the unaccustomed brightness
Of the winter dawning, the strange unheavenly glare :
The eye marvelled—marvelled at the dazzling whiteness ; 15
   The ear hearkened to the stillness of the solemn air ;
No sound of wheel rumbling nor of foot falling,
And the busy morning cries came thin and spare.
   Then boys I heard, as they went to school, calling,
They gathered up the crystal manna to freeze   20
Their tongues with tasting, their hands with snow-balling ;
   Or rioted in a drift, plunging up to the knees ;
Or peering up from under the white-mossed wonder,
" O look at the trees ! " they cried, " O look at the trees ! "

With lessened load a few carts creak and blunder, 25
Following along the white deserted way,
A country company long dispersed asunder:
  When now already the sun, in pale display
Standing by Paul's high dome, spread forth below
His sparkling beams, and awoke the stir of the day. 30
  For now doors open, and war is waged with the snow;
And trains of sombre men, past tale of number,
Tread long brown paths, as toward their toil they go:
  But even for them awhile no cares encumber
Their minds diverted; the daily word is unspoken, 35
The daily thoughts of labour and sorrow slumber
At the sight of the beauty that greets them, for the charm they have broken.

ROBERT BRIDGES
(*20th Century*)

1. Lines 1-12. A perfect description of falling snow.

    (*a*) Note the words describing the falling flakes.
    (*b*) Note the words suggesting how silently they fall and how they produce silence.
    (*c*) Note how the rhythm suggests falling snow.
    (*d*) Note how the rhyme scheme, the most interesting in this book, also suggests falling snow.

2. Line 13. Where do you see this brightness first when there has been a heavy snowfall during the night?

3. Explain line 16.

4. Lines 19-24. You all know this picture.

5. Lines 32-37. In what way does this differ from, and in what way does it resemble, the picture in lines 19-24?

Notes: page 182.

WHEN ICICLES HANG BY THE WALL

When icicles hang by the wall,
  And Dick the shepherd blows his nail,
And Tom bears logs into the hall,
  And milk comes frozen home in pail,
When blood is nipp'd, and ways be foul,   5
Then nightly sings the staring owl,
Tuwhit! tuwhoo! A merry note!
While greasy Joan doth keel the pot.

When all aloud the wind doth blow,   10
  And coughing drowns the parson's saw,
And birds sit brooding in the snow,
  And Marian's nose looks red and raw,
When roasted crabs hiss in the bowl
Then nightly sings the staring owl,   15
Tuwhit! tuwhoo! A merry note!
While greasy Joan doth keel the pot.

                    SHAKESPEARE
                    (1564-1616)

1. Compare this poem with "London Snow", and note:

    (*a*) the difference in scene;
    (*b*) the difference in the manner in which the writers regard winter.

2. In what ways do lines 1-5 resemble lines 10-14?

3. How would you read "tuwhoo"?

4. Why is it called a "merry" note? Would it be better to call it an "eerie" note?

5. In which poem do you feel the cold more? Why?

Notes: page 182.

From FROST AT MIDNIGHT

Therefore all seasons shall be sweet to thee,
Whether the summer clothe the general earth
With greenness, or the redbreast sit and sing
Betwixt the tufts of snow on the bare branch
Of mossy apple-tree, while the nigh thatch   5
Smokes in the sun-thaw; whether the eave-drops fall
Heard only in the trances of the blast,
Or if the secret ministry of frost
Shall hang them up in silent icicles,
Quietly shining to the quiet moon.   10

COLERIDGE
(1772-1834)

1. Count the pictures in these ten lines.

2. One of these is purely a "sound" picture. Which is the most effective word in it?

3. Lines 8-10. What makes this picture seem so peaceful? What are the effective words in it?

4. Which seems to you the best instance of the effective use of language (*i.e.* of saying much in few words) in this poem?

5. Which picture do you like best?

Notes: page 183.

THE PARROTS

Somewhere, somewhen I've seen,
But where or when I'll never know,
Parrots of shrilly green
With crests of shriller scarlet flying
Out of black cedars as the sun was dying   5
Against cold peaks of snow.

From what forgotten life
Of other worlds I cannot tell
Flashes that screeching strife:
Yet the shrill colour and shrill crying   10
Sing through my blood and set my heart replying
And jangling like a bell.

W. W. GIBSON
(20*th Century*)

1. Stanza 1. Read this stanza, omitting the second line. What do you lose?

2. Note the colours—green, scarlet, black, white, in the sunset light. Are the words " shrilly " and " shriller " appropriate?

3. When you think of the picture in stanza 1, where is the sun, where are the peaks, the cedars, the parrots, and where are you?

4. What is meant exactly by " screeching strife " in line 9?

5. What does the second stanza give us that is not in the first?

6. Do lines 10 and 11 tell you how to read the poem?

   Notes: page 183.

TWO PEWITS

Under the after-sunset sky
Two pewits sport and cry,
More white than is the moon on high
Riding the dark surge silently;
More black than earth. Their cry   5
Is the one sound under the sky.
They alone move, now low, now high,
And merrily they cry
To the mischievous Spring sky,
Plunging earthward, tossing high,   10
Over the ghost who wonders why
So merrily they cry and fly,
Nor choose 'twixt earth and sky,
While the moon's quarter silently
Rides, and earth rests as silently.   15

EDWARD THOMAS
(*20th Century*)

1. How do the words used for rhyming in this poem suggest the cry and the flight of the birds? Note that "sky" occurs four times, "cry" three times, "high" three times, "silently" three times, and "why" and "fly" each once.

2. Do lines 3 and 5 contradict each other?

3. Why are the words "riding" and "silently" in line 4 particularly suitable?

4. Who is the ghost referred to in line 11?

5. What is the most striking difference between this poem and the last?

6. Compare this poem with the previous one. Which can you see the clearer, the parrots or the pewits?

7. How do the words "sport", "mischievous", "merrily", affect the atmosphere of the poem?

8. Can you see the picture?

Notes: page 184.

DUCKS

I

From troubles of the world
I turn to ducks,
Beautiful comical things
Sleeping or curled
Their heads beneath white wings
By water cool,
Or finding curious things
To eat in various mucks
Beneath the pool,
Tails uppermost, or waddling
Sailor-like on the shores
Of ponds, or paddling
—Left! right!—with fanlike feet
Which are for steady oars
When they (white galleys) float
Each bird a boat
Rippling at will the sweet
Wide waterway . . .

When night is fallen *you* creep
Upstairs, but drakes and dillies
Nest with pale water-stars,
Moonbeams and shadow bars,
And water-lilies:
Fearful too much to sleep
Since they've no locks
To click against the teeth
Of weasel and fox.
And warm beneath
Are eggs of cloudy green
Whence hungry rats and lean
Would stealthily suck
New life, but for the mien,
The bold ferocious mien
Of the mother-duck.

II

Yes, ducks are valiant things
On nests of twigs and straws,
And ducks are soothy things
And lovely on the lake
When that the sunlight draws
Thereon their pictures dim
In colours cool.
And when beneath the pool
They dabble, and when they swim
And make their rippling rings,
O ducks are beautiful things!

But ducks are comical things:
As comical as you.
Quack!
They waddle round, they do.
They eat all sorts of things,
And then they quack.
By barn and stable and stack
They wander at their will,
But if you go too near
They look at you through black
Small topaz-tinted eyes
And wish you ill.
Triangular and clear
They leave their curious track
In mud at the water's edge,
And there amid the sedge
And slime they gobble and peer
Saying, " Quack! quack! "

III

When God had finished the stars and whirl of coloured suns
He turned His mind from big things to fashion little ones,
Beautiful tiny things (like daisies) He made, and then
He made the comical ones in case the minds of men
    Should stiffen and become
    Dull, humourless and glum:
And so forgetful of their Maker be
As to take even themselves—*quite seriously*.
Caterpillars and cats are lively and excellent puns:
All God's jokes are good—even the practical ones!
And as for the duck, I think God must have smiled a bit
Seeing those bright eyes blink on the day He fashioned it.
And He's probably laughing still at the sound that came out of its bill!

F. W. HARVEY
(20th Century)

1. Perhaps the most charming thing in this poem is the blending of the beautiful and the comical.
   - (*a*) Which is the most beautiful picture in parts I and II?
   - (*b*) Which is the most comical picture in parts I and II?

2. In most of the pictures here the ducks are in or near the water, and we seem to feel its coolness. In how many is there no suggestion of water?

3. Do you remember the poem of the " Merry Heart " (" Jog on, jog on," etc.)? In what way does part III confirm it?

4. What lines in part I contain the main idea of part III?

5. Compare with the last two poems. Which do you see most clearly, parrots, pewits, or ducks?

Notes: page 185.

THE SKYLARK

    Bird of the wilderness,
    Blithesome and cumberless,
Sweet be thy matin o'er moorland and lea!
    Emblem of happiness,
    Blest is thy dwelling-place— 5
Oh, to abide in the desert with thee!

    Wild is thy lay and loud;
    Far in the downy cloud,
Love gives it energy, love gave it birth.
    Where, on thy dewy wing, 10
    Where art thou journeying?
Thy lay is in heaven, thy love is on earth.

    O'er fell and fountain sheen,
    O'er moor and mountain green,
O'er the red streamer that heralds the day, 15
    Over the cloudlet dim,
    Over the rainbow's rim,
Musical cherub, soar, singing, away!

    Then, when the gloaming comes,
    Low in the heather blooms 20
Sweet will thy welcome and bed of love be!
    Emblem of happiness,
    Blest is thy dwelling-place—
Oh, to abide in the desert with thee!

                        HOGG
                      (1770-1835)

1. Do you see the skylark as clearly as the ducks in the previous poem?
2. In what is the poet here chiefly interested?
3. Compare the rhythm of this poem with that of "Ducks". Which do you prefer?
4. There are four stanzas here and three different rhyme schemes.

Notes: page 185.

TO A SKYLARK

Ethereal minstrel! pilgrim of the sky!
  Dost thou despise the earth where cares abound?
Or, while the wings aspire, are heart and eye
  Both with thy nest upon the dewy ground?
Thy nest which thou canst drop into at will,   5
Those quivering wings composed, that music still.

To the last point of vision, and beyond,
  Mount, daring warbler! that love prompted strain
('Twixt thee and thine a never-failing bond)
  Thrills not the less the bosom of the plain: 10
Yet might'st thou seem, proud privilege! to sing
All independent of the leafy spring.

Leave to the nightingale her shady wood;
  A privacy of glorious light is thine,
Whence thou dost pour upon the world a flood   15
  Of harmony, with instinct more divine;
Type of the wise who soar, but never roam;
True to the kindred points of heaven and home.

                        WORDSWORTH
                        (1770-1850)

1. Is the picture of the skylark becoming clearer? See question 1, page 86.
2. In what is the poet chiefly interested?
3. The two poems on the skylark were written over a hundred years ago. "Ducks", "The Parrots", and "Two Pewits" are all by modern poets. Here is a stanza from another poem on the skylark:

> *Higher still and higher*
>   *From the earth thou springest*
> *Like a cloud of fire;*
>   *The blue deep thou wingest,*
> *And singing still dost soar, and soaring ever singest.*

  To which group do you think this belongs?

4. Compare the rhythm of this poem with that of the last. Which suggests more clearly the flight of the skylark?
5. Are these two poems on the skylark disappointing because they do not describe the bird?

Notes: page 185.

THE TIGER

Tiger, tiger, burning bright
In the forests of the night,
What immortal hand or eye
Could frame thy fearful symmetry?

In what distant deeps or skies   5
Burnt the fire of thine eyes?
On what wings dare he aspire?
What the hand dare seize the fire?

And what shoulder and what art
Could twist the sinews of thy heart?   10
And, when thy heart began to beat,
What dread hand and what dread feet?

What the hammer? What the chain?
In what furnace was thy brain?
What the anvil? What dread grasp   15
Dare its deadly terrors clasp?

When the stars threw down their spears,
And watered heaven with their tears,
Did He smile His work to see?
Did He who made the lamb make thee?   20

Tiger, tiger, burning bright
In the forests of the night,
What immortal hand or eye
Dare frame thy fearful symmetry?

BLAKE
(1757-1827)

1. How would you describe Blake's feelings with regard to the tiger?
2. How would you answer the questions in lines **19 and 20**?
3. Why is "could" in the fourth line changed to "dare" in the last line?

Notes: page 186.

HERVÉ RIEL

I

On the sea and at the Hogue, sixteen hundred ninety-two,
   Did the English fight the French—woe to France!
And, the thirty-first of May, helter-skelter through the blue,
Like a crowd of frightened porpoises a shoal of sharks
      pursue,
   Came crowding ship on ship to Saint-Malo, on the Rance,   5
With the English fleet in view.

II

'Twas the squadron that escaped, with the victor in full
      chase;
   First and foremost of the drove, in his great ship,
      Damfreville;
      Close on him fled, great and small,
      Twenty-two good ships in all;   10
And they signalled to the place
"Help the winners of a race!
   Get us guidance, give us harbour, take us quick—or,
      quicker still,
   Here's the English can and will!"

III

Then the pilots of the place put out brisk and leapt on board;
  "Why, what hope or chance have ships like these to pass?" laughed they:
"Rocks to starboard, rocks to port, all the passage scarred and scored—
Shall the *Formidable* here, with her twelve and eighty guns,
  Think to make the river-mouth by the single narrow way,
Trust to enter—where 'tis ticklish for a craft of twenty tons,
  And with flow at full beside?
  Now, 'tis slackest ebb of tide.
  Reach the mooring? Rather say,
While rock stands or water runs,
  Not a ship will leave the bay!"

IV

Then was called a council straight.
Brief and bitter the debate:
"Here's the English at our heels; would you have them take in tow
All that's left us of the fleet, linked together stern and bow,
For a prize to Plymouth Sound?
Better run the ships aground!"
    (Ended Damfreville his speech.)
"Not a minute more to wait!
  Let the Captains all and each
    Shove ashore, then blow up, burn the vessels on the beach!
France must undergo her fate.

V

Give the word!" But no such word
Was ever spoke or heard;
  For up stood, for out stepped, for in struck amid all
     these
—A Captain? A Lieutenant? A Mate—first, second,
     third?   40
  No such man of mark, and meet
  With his betters to compete!
But a simple Breton sailor pressed by Tourville for the
     fleet,
A poor coasting-pilot he, Hervé Riel the Croisickese.

VI

And "What mockery or malice have we here?" cries
     Hervé Riel: 45
  "Are you mad, you Malouins? Are you cowards,
     fools, or rogues?
Talk to me of rocks and shoals, me who took the soundings,
     tell
On my fingers every bank, every shallow, every swell
  'Twixt the offing here and Grève where the river
     disembogues?
Are you bought by English gold? Is it love the lying's
     for?   50
  Morn and eve, night and day,
  Have I piloted your bay,
Entered free and anchored fast at the foot of Solidor.
  Burn the fleet and ruin France? That were worse than
     fifty Hogues!
      Sirs, they know I speak the truth! Sirs, believe
        me there's a way!   55

Only let me lead the line,
  Have the biggest ship to steer,
  Get this *Formidable* clear,
Make the others follow mine,
And I lead them, most and least, by a passage I know well, 60
  Right to Solidor past Grève,
    And there lay them safe and sound;
  And if one ship misbehave—
    Keel so much as grate the ground,
Why, I've nothing but my life—here's my head! cries Hervé Riel.

65

VII

Not a minute more to wait.
"Steer us in, then, small and great!
  Take the helm, lead the line, save the squadron!"
    cried its chief.
Captains, give the sailor place!
  He is Admiral, in brief.
Still the north-wind, by God's grace! 70
See the noble fellow's face
As the big ship, with a bound,
Clears the entry like a hound,
Keeps the passage, as its inch of way were the wide sea's profound!
  See, safe through shoal and rock, 75
  How they follow in a flock,
Not a ship that misbehaves, not a keel that grates the ground,
  Not a spar that comes to grief!
The peril, see, is past.
All are harboured to the last, 80
And just as Hervé Riel hollas "Anchor!"—sure as fate,
Up the English come—too late!

VIII

So, the storm subsides to calm:
    They see the green trees wave
    On the heights o'erlooking Grève.
Hearts that bled are staunched with balm.
    Just our rapture to enhance,
    Let the English rake the bay,
Gnash their teeth and glare askance
    As they cannonade away!
'Neath rampired Solidor pleasant riding on the Rance!"
How hope succeeds despair on each Captain's countenance!
Out burst all with one accord,
    "This is Paradise for Hell!
    Let France, let France's King
Thank the man that did the thing!"
What a shout, and all one word,
    "Hervé Riel!"
As he stepped in front once more,
    Not a symptom of surprise
    In the frank blue Breton eyes,
Just the same man as before.

IX

Then said Damfreville, "My friend,
I must speak out at the end,
    Though I find the speaking hard.
Praise is deeper than the lips:
You have saved the King his ships,
    You must name your own reward.
'Faith our sun was near eclipse!
Demand whate'er you will,
France remains your debtor still.
Ask to heart's content and have! or my name's not Damfreville."

X

Then a beam of fun outbroke
On the bearded mouth that spoke, 115
As the honest heart laughed through
Those frank eyes of Breton blue:
" Since I needs must say my say,
  Since on board the duty's done,
  And from Malo Roads to Croisic Point, what is it but
      a run?— 120
Since 'tis ask and have, I may—
  Since the others go ashore—
Come! a good whole holiday!
  Leave to go and see my wife, whom I call the Belle
      Aurore!"
That he asked and that he got—nothing more. 125

XI

Name and deed alike are lost:
Not a pillar nor a post
  In his Croisic keeps alive the feat as it befell;
Not a head in white and black
On a single fishing-smack, 130
In memory of the man but for whom had gone to wrack
  All that France saved from the fight whence England
      bore the bell.
Go to Paris: rank on rank
  Search the heroes flung pell-mell
On the Louvre, face and flank! 135
  You shall look long enough ere you come to Hervé Riel.

So, for better and for worse,
Hervé Riel, accept my verse!
In my verse, Hervé Riel, do thou once more
Save the squadron, honour France, love thy wife the
      Belle Aurore!   140

BROWNING
(1812-1889)

The story the poem records is true.

1. Stanzas I and II. Have you noticed how the rhythm here helps you to feel the hurry and excitement of the chase? Compare with "San Stefano", page 11.

2. Stanza III. Why did the pilots refuse?

3. Stanza IV. Compare this stanza with what actually happened to Tourville, the Admiral of the fleet in this battle. He had escaped with thirteen great ships into Cherbourg. But, to let their own crews escape, the ships had to be run ashore. The English then sent in their boats and burned the ships before the eyes of the French. Was this to happen to the remainder of the fleet, the squadron under Damfreville?

4. Stanza VI (last three lines). Is there any need for Hervé Riel to offer his life?

5. Stanza VII, line 71. What does this line mean?

6. Stanza VII, lines 82-83. What do these lines mean?

7. Stanza VIII, lines 88-92. Who are speaking here?

8. Stanza X. Why did Hervé Riel not ask for more?

9. If you have answered the last question find a line in Damfreville's speech in Stanza IX which seems to contain the meaning of the poem.

Notes: page 186.

LUCY ASHTON'S SONG

Look not thou on beauty's charming;
Sit thou still when kings are arming;
Taste not when the wine-cup glistens;
Speak not when the people listens;
Stop thine ear against the singer; 5
From the red gold keep thy finger;
Vacant heart and hand and eye,
Easy live and quiet die.

SCOTT
(1771-1832)

THE REPLY

Sound, sound the clarion, fill the fife!
  To all the sensual world proclaim,
One crowded hour of glorious life
  Is worth an age without a name.

1. Why do you think I put these two little poems after "Hervé Riel"?
2. To which stanza of "Hervé Riel" does the third line of "The Reply" apply perfectly?
3. "The Reply", formerly attributed to Scott, is now attributed to Major Mordaunt.

Notes: page 187.

THE YERL O' WATERYDECK

The wind it blew, and the ship it flew,
　And it was " Hey for hame ! "
But up an' cried the skipper til his crew,
　" Haud her oot ower the saut sea faem."

Syne up an' spak the angry king:　　　　　　　5
　" Haud on for Dumferline ! "
Quo' the skipper, " My lord, this maunna be—
　I'm king on this boat o' mine ! "

He tuik the helm intil his han',
　He left the shore un'er the lee ;　　　　　　10
Syne croodit sail, an', east an' south,
　Stude awa, richt oot to sea.

Quo' the king, " Leise-majesty, I trow !
　Here lies some ill-set plan !
'Bout ship ! " Quo' the skipper, " Your grace forgets　　15
　Ye are king but o' the lan' ! "

Oot he heild to the open sea
　While the north wind flaughtered an' fell ;
Syne the east had a bitter word to say
　That waukent a watery hell.　　　　　　　20

He turnt her heid intil the north:
  Quo' the nobles, "He s' droon, by the mass!"
Quo' the skipper, "Haud aff your lady han's
  Or ye'll never see the Bass."

The king creepit down the cabin-stair　　　25
  To drink the gude French wine;
An' up cam' his dochter, the princess fair,
  An' luikit ower the brine.

She turnt her face to the drivin' snaw
  To the snaw but and the weet;　　　30
It claucht her snood, an' awa' like a clood
  Her hair drave oot i' the sleet.

She turnt her face frae the drivin' win'—
  "What's that aheid?" quo' she.
The skipper he threw himsel frae the win'　　　35
  An' he brayt the helm alee.

"Put to your han', my lady fair!
  Haud up her heid!" quo' he;
"Gin she dinna face the win' a wee mair
  It's fareweel to you an' me!"　　　40

To the tiller the lady she laid her han',
  An' the ship brayt her cheek to the blast;
They joukit the berg, but her quarter scraped,
  An' they luikit at ither aghast.

Quo' the skipper, "Ye are a lady fair, 45
  An' a princess gran' to see,
But were ye a beggar, a man wud sail
  To the hell i' your company!"

She liftit a pale an' a queenly face,
  Her een flashed, an' syne they swam: 50
"An' what for no to the heaven?" she says,
  An' she turnt awa' frae him.

But she tuik na her han' frae the gude ship's helm
  Till the day began to daw;
An' the skipper he spak, but what was said 55
  It was said atween them twa.

An' syne the gude ship she lay to,
  Wi' Scotlan' hyne un'er the lee;
An' the king cam' up the cabin-stair
  Wi' wan face an' bluidshot ee. 60

Laigh loutit the skipper upo' the deck;
  "Stan' up, stan' up," quo' the king;
"Ye're an honest loun—an' beg me a boon
  When ye gie me back this ring."

Lowne blew the win'; the stars cam' oot; 65
  The ship turnt frae the north;
An' or ever the sun was up an' aboot
  They were intil the firth o' Forth.

When the gude ship lay at the pier-heid,
   And the king stude steady o' the lan'—   70
"Doon wi' ye, skipper—doon!" he said,
   "Hoo daur ye afore me stan'!"

The skipper he loutit on his knee;
   The king his blade he drew:
Quo' the king, "Noo mynt ye to contre me!   75
   I'm aboord *my* vessel noo!

"Gin I hadna been your verra gude lord
   I wud hae thrawn yer neck!
But—ye wha loutit Skipper o' Doon,
   Rise up Yerl o' Waterydeck."   80

The skipper he rasena: "Your Grace is great,
   Your will it can heize or ding:
Wi' ae wee word ye hae made me a yerl—
   Wi' anither mak' me a king."

"I canna mak' ye a king," quo' he,   85
   "The Lord alane can do that!
I snowk leise-majesty, my man!
   What the Sathan wad ye be at?"

Glowert at the skipper the doutsum king
   Jalousin' aneth his croon;   90
Quo' the skipper, "Here is your Grace's ring,
   An' your dochter is my boon!"

The black blude shot intil the king's face—
  He wasna bonny to see:
"The rascal skipper! he lichtlies oor grace!—   95
  Gar hang him high on yon tree."

Up sprang the skipper an' aboord his ship,
  Cleikit up a bitin' blade
And hackit at the cable that held her to the pier,
  An' thoucht it 'maist ower weel made.   100

The king he blew shrill in a siller whustle;
  An' tramp, tramp, doon the pier
Cam' twenty men on twenty horses,
  Clankin' wi' spur an' spear.

At the king's foot fell his dochter fair: 105
  "His life ye wadna spill!"
"Ye daur stan' 'twixt my hert an' my hate?"
  "I daur, wi' a richt gude will!"

"Ye was aye to your faither a thrawart bairn,
  But, my lady, here stan's the king!   110
Luikna *him* i' the angry face—
  A monarch's anither thing!"

"I lout to my father for his grace
  Low on my bendit knee;
But I stan' an' luik the king i' the face,   115
  For the skipper is king o' me!"

She turnt, she sprang upo' the deck,
  The cable splashed i' the Forth,
Her wings sae braid the gude ship spread
  And flew east, an' syne flew north.   120

Now was not this a king's dochter—
  A lady that feared no skaith?
A woman wi' wham a man micht sail
  Prood intil the Port o' Death?

GEORGE MACDONALD
(1824-1905)

Permission has been granted to modify the original Old Scots form of certain words.

heild : *held*
flaughtered : *fluttered*
he s' droon : *he 'll drown*
claucht : *caught*
snood : *hair-band*
brayt : *pushed*
joukit : *dodged*
wud : *would*
daw : *dawn*
syne : *then*
hyne : *far away*
laigh : *low*
loutit : *bowed*
loun : *fellow*

lowne : *gently*
mynt : *try*
contre : *oppose*
thrawn : *wrung*
heize : *raise up*
ding : *cast down*
snowk : *smell*
glowert : *glared*
doutsom : *suspicious*
jalousin' : *questioning*
lichtlies : *slights*
cleikit : *snatched*
thrawart : *obstinate*

1. Lines 1–24. Compare the skipper with the boatswain in the passage from "The Tempest" on page 103.
2. Lines 33–36. The skipper is at the helm. Why does the princess see the iceberg first?
3. Line 61. Why is the skipper so humble now?
4. Line 100. Did he ever think that before?
5. Compare lines 109–112 with lines 113–116.

   Notes: page 187.

From THE TEMPEST

(The King of Naples and his courtiers are aboard this ship. There is a storm with thunder and lightning. The Boatswain encourages his men.)

Act I, Scene I

Boats.—Heigh, my hearts! cheerly, cheerly, my hearts! yare, yare: take in the topsail! Tend to the master's whistle. Blow, till thou burst thy wind, if room enough!

Enter Alonso, Antonio, Gonzalo, and others.

Alon.—Good boatswain, have care. Where's the master? Play the men.
Boats.—I pray now, keep below.
Ant.—Where is the master, boatswain?
Boats.—Do you not hear him? You mar our labour: keep your cabins: you do assist the storm.
Gon.—Nay, good, be patient.
Boats.—When the sea is. Hence! What cares these roarers for the name of king? To cabin: silence! trouble us not.
Gon.—Good, yet remember whom thou hast aboard.
Boats.—None that I more love than myself. You are a counsellor; if you can command these elements to silence, and work the peace of the present, we will not hand a rope more; use your authority: if you cannot, give thanks you have lived so long, and make yourself ready in your cabin for the mischance of the hour, if it so hap.—Cheerly, good hearts.—Out of our way, I say.

SHAKESPEARE
(1564–1616)

1. The boatswain here is a man of the same stamp as the skipper in the last poem. Which lines show his character most clearly?
Notes: page 187.

OPEN THE DOOR TO ME, OH!

Oh, open the door, some pity to shew,
  Oh, open the door to me, Oh!
Tho' thou hast been false, I'll ever prove true—
  Oh, open the door to me, Oh!

Cauld is the blast upon my pale cheek,   5
  But caulder thy love for me, Oh!
The frost that freezes the life at my heart
  Is nought to my pains frae thee, Oh!

The wan moon is setting behind the white wave,
  And time is setting with me, Oh!   10
False friends, false love, farewell! for mair
  I'll ne'er trouble them nor thee, Oh!

She has open'd the door, she has open'd it wide,
  She sees the pale corse on the plain, Oh!
My true love, she cried, and sank down by his side,   15
  Never to rise again, Oh!

BURNS
(1759-1796)

1. This little song is very like an old ballad. Compare it with the next poem and you will see this.

2. Stanza 1. Note the amount of repetition in this stanza. Do you like it? Compare the following from Coleridge:

   Alone, alone, all, all alone,
   Alone on a wide wide sea.

   See also the first stanza of "Will Ye no' Come Back Again?" (page 136).

3. Which stanza do you prefer?

   Notes: page 188.

TO ALTHEA FROM PRISON

When Love with unconfinéd wings
   Hovers within my gates,
And my divine Althea brings
   To whisper at the grates;
When I lie tangled in her hair   5
   And fetter'd to her eye,
The birds that wanton in the air
   Know no such liberty.

When flowing cups run swiftly round
   With no allaying Thames,   10
Our careless heads with roses bound,
   Our hearts with loyal flames;
When thirsty grief in wine we steep,
   When healths and draughts go free—
Fishes that tipple in the deep   15
   Know no such liberty.

When, like committed linnets, I
   With shriller throat shall sing
The sweetness, mercy, majesty,
   And glories of my King;   20
When I shall voice aloud how good
   He is, how great should be,
Enlargéd winds, that curl the flood,
   Know no such liberty.

>   Stone walls do not a prison make,   25
>   Nor iron bars a cage;
>   Minds innocent and quiet take
>   That for an hermitage;
>   If I have freedom in my love
>   And in my soul am free,   30
>   Angels alone, that soar above,
>   Enjoy such liberty.

LOVELACE
(1618-1658)

1. Compare the atmosphere of this poem with that of the last.

2. If we say the first stanza deals with love, what might we say the second deals with, and what the third?

3. Suggest a name for the poem that would apply to all four stanzas.

4. In line 25 you find the main idea of the poem expressed. This is what we call a paradox. Wordsworth's line, " The child is father of the man ", is another example. Are there any others in the poem?

5. Of the first three stanzas which as a whole forms the best paradox?

6. Lines 9-10. Shakespeare makes an old Roman say that he is " one that loves a cup of hot wine with not a drop of allaying Tiber in't."

7. Which lines in the poem do you like best?

Notes: page 188.

MARY MORISON

O Mary, at thy window be,
  It is the wish'd, the trysted hour!
Those smiles and glances let me see,
  That make the miser's treasure poor:
How blythely wad I bide the stoure,
  A weary slave frae sun to sun;
Could I the rich reward secure,
  The lovely Mary Morison.

Yestreen, when to the trembling string
  The dance gaed thro' the lighted ha',
To thee my fancy took its wing,
  I sat, but neither heard nor saw:
Tho' this was fair, and that was braw,
  And yon the toast of a' the town,
I sigh'd, and said amang them a',
  "Ye are na Mary Morison."

Oh, Mary, canst thou wreck his peace,
  Wha for thy sake wad gladly die?
Or canst thou break that heart of his,
  Whase only faut is loving thee?
If love for love thou wilt na gie,
  At least be pity to me shown;
A thought ungentle canna be
  The thought o' Mary Morison.

BURNS
(1759-1796)

1. Compare this poem with "Open the Door to Me, Oh!" Is this poem like an old ballad?
2. Which stanza do you like best?
3. What is the finest compliment he pays to Mary?

Notes: page 188.

THE HIGHWAYMAN

Part I

The wind was a torrent of darkness among the gusty trees,
The moon was a ghostly galleon tossed upon cloudy seas,
The road was a ribbon of moonlight over the purple moor,
And the highwayman came riding—
    Riding—riding— 5
The highwayman came riding, up to the old inn-door.

He'd a French cocked hat on his forehead, a bunch of lace at his chin,
A coat of the claret velvet, and breeches of brown doeskin;
They fitted with never a wrinkle: his boots were up to the thigh.
And he rode with a jewelled twinkle, 10
    His pistol butts a-twinkle,
His rapier hilt a-twinkle, under the jewelled sky.

Over the cobbles he clattered and clashed in the dark inn-yard,
And he tapped with his whip on the shutters, but all was locked and barred;
He whistled a tune to the window, and who should be waiting there 15
But the landlord's black-eyed daughter,
    Bess, the landlord's daughter,
Plaiting a dark red love-knot into her long black hair.

And dark in the dark old inn-yard a stable wicket creaked
Where Tim the ostler listened; his face was white and   20
    peaked;
His eyes were hollows of madness, his hair like mouldy hay,
But he loved the landlord's daughter,
       The landlord's red-lipped daughter,
Dumb as a dog he listened, and he heard the robber say—

" One kiss, my bonny sweetheart, I'm after a prize   25
    to-night,
But I shall be back with the yellow gold before the morning light;
Yet, if they press me sharply, and harry me through the day,
Then look for me by moonlight,
       Watch for me by moonlight,
I'll come to thee by moonlight, though hell should   30
    bar the way."

He rose upright in the stirrups; he scarce could reach her hand,
But she loosened her hair i' the casement. His face burnt like a brand
As the black cascade of perfume came tumbling over his breast;
And he kissed its waves in the moonlight,
       (Oh sweet black waves in the moonlight!)   35
Then he tugged at his rein in the moonlight, and galloped away to the west.

Part II

He did not come in the dawning; he did not come at noon;
And out o' the tawny sunset, before the rise o' the moon,
When the road was a gypsy's ribbon, looping the purple moor,
A red-coat troop came marching—   40
    Marching—marching—
King George's men came marching up to the old inn-door.

They said no word to the landlord, they drank his ale instead,
But they gagged his daughter and bound her to the foot of her narrow bed;
Two of them knelt at her casement, with muskets at their side.   45
There was death at every window;
    And hell at one dark window;
For Bess could see, through her casement, the road that *he* would ride.

They had tied her up to attention, with many a sniggering jest;
They had bound a musket beside her, with the barrel beneath her breast.   50
"Now keep good watch!" and they kissed her.
    She heard the dead man say—
Look for me by moonlight;
    Watch for me by moonlight;
I'll come to thee by moonlight, though hell should bar the way!

She twisted her hands behind her; but all the knots 55
   held good.
She writhed her hands till her fingers were wet with
   sweat or blood.
They stretched and strained in the darkness, and the
   hours crawled by like years,
Till, now, on the stroke of midnight,
      Cold, on the stroke of midnight,
The tip of one finger touched it! The trigger at 60
   least was hers!

The tip of one finger touched it; she strove no more
   for the rest.
Up, she stood up to attention, with the barrel beneath
   her breast.
She would not risk their hearing; she would not
   strive again;
For the road lay bare in the moonlight;
      Blank and bare in the moonlight; 65
And the blood of her veins in the moonlight throbbed
   to her love's refrain.

Tlot-tlot, tlot-tlot! Had they heard it? The horse-
   hoofs ringing clear;
Tlot-tlot, tlot-tlot, in the distance? Were they deaf
   that they did not hear?
Down the ribbon of moonlight, over the brow of the
   hill,
The highwayman came riding, 70
      Riding, riding!
The red-coats looked to their priming. She stood up,
   straight and still.

Tlot-tlot, in the frosty silence! *Tlot-tlot*, in the echoing night!
Nearer he came and nearer. Her face was like a light.
Her eyes grew wide for a moment; she drew one last deep breath,   75
Then her finger moved in the moonlight,
    Her musket shattered the moonlight,
Shattered her breast in the moonlight and warned him—with her death.

He turned; he spurred to the westward; he did not know who stood
Bowed, with her head o'er the musket, drenched with her own red blood!   80
Not till the dawn he heard it, and slowly blanched to hear
How Bess, the landlord's daughter,
    The landlord's black-eyed daughter,
Had watched for her love in the moonlight, and died in the darkness there.

Back he spurred like a madman, shrieking a curse to the sky,   85
With the white road smoking behind him, and his rapier brandished high.
Blood-red were his spurs i' the golden noon; wine-red was his velvet coat;
When they shot him down on the highway,
    Down like a dog on the highway;
And he lay in his blood on the highway, with the bunch of lace at his throat.   90

*And still of a winter's night, they say, when the wind is
    in the trees,*
When the moon is a ghostly galleon tossed upon cloudy seas,
*When the road is a ribbon of moonlight over the purple
    moor,*
A highwayman comes riding—
    Riding—riding— 95
A highwayman comes riding, up to the old inn-door.

*Over the cobbles he clatters and clangs in the dark
    inn-yard,*
*And he taps with his whip on the shutters, but all is
    locked and barred;*
*He whistles a tune to the window, and who should be
    waiting there*
But the landlord's black-eyed daughter, 100
    Bess, the landlord's daughter,
Plaiting a dark red love-knot into her long black hair.

ALFRED NOYES
(20*th Century*)

1. What does the rhythm of this poem suggest?
2. Stanza 1. What would be the effect of omitting lines 4 and 5?
3. When is the wind a "torrent of darkness"?
4. When is the moon most like a "ghostly galleon"?
5. In which stanza did you feel the most complete satisfaction?
6. If you had to paint two, and only two, pictures to illustrate this poem, which would you choose?
7. Both Bess and her lover die in the poem, and yet we do not feel sad. Why?
8. What is especially interesting about the last two stanzas?

Notes: page 189.

SILVER

Slowly, silently, now the moon
Walks the night in her silver shoon;
This way, and that, she peers, and sees
Silver fruit upon silver trees;
One by one the casements catch 5
Her beams beneath the silvery thatch;
Couched in his kennel, like a log,
With paws of silver sleeps the dog;
From their shadowy cote the white breasts peep
Of doves in a silver-feathered sleep; 10
A harvest mouse goes scampering by,
With silver claws, and silver eye;
And moveless fish in the water gleam,
By silver reeds in a silver stream.

WALTER DE LA MARE
(*20th Century*)

1. How would you read this poem?

2. What is the effect of line 11?

3. Compare the atmosphere of this poem with that of "The Listeners", page 16.

Notes: page 189.

SOME MOON PICTURES FROM THE POETS

(1)   I walk unseen
On the dry smooth-shaven Green,
To behold the wand'ring Moon,
Riding neer her highest noon,
Like one that had bin led astray,   5
Through the Heav'ns wide pathles way;
And oft, as if her head she bow'd,
Stooping through a fleecy cloud.

MILTON

(2) The Moon, like a flower,
In heaven's high bower,
With silent delight
Sits and smiles on the night.

BLAKE

(3) The Moon doth with delight
Look round her when the heavens are bare.

WORDSWORTH

(4) Yon crescent Moon as fixed as if it grew
In its own cloudless starless lake of blue.

COLERIDGE

(5) The moving Moon went up the sky,
And nowhere did abide;
Softly she was going up,
And a star or two beside.

COLERIDGE

This last stanza is from "The Ancient Mariner". Beside it Coleridge puts the following description in prose.

(6) In his loneliness and fixedness he yearneth towards
the journeying Moon, and the stars that still sojourn,
yet still move onward; and everywhere the blue
sky belongs to them, and is their appointed rest, and
their native country and their own natural homes,
which they enter unannounced, as lords that are
certainly expected and yet there is a silent joy at
their arrival.

COLERIDGE

(7)   The Moon lifting her silver rim
Above a cloud, and with a gradual swim
Coming into the blue with all her light.

KEATS

(8) THE ASCENT OF SNOWDON

It was a close, warm, breezeless summer night,
Wan, dull, and glaring, with a dripping fog
Low-hung and thick that covered all the sky;
But, undiscouraged, we began to climb
The mountain-side. . . .   5
                With forehead bent
Earthward, as if in opposition set
Against an enemy, I panted up
With eager pace, and no less eager thoughts.
Thus might we wear a midnight hour away,   10
Ascending at loose distance each from each,
And I, as chanced, the foremost of the band;
When at my feet the ground appeared to brighten,
And with a step or two seemed brighter still;
Nor was time given to ask or learn the cause,   15
For instantly a light upon the turf
Fell like a flash, and lo! as I looked up,
The Moon hung naked in a firmament
Of azure without cloud, and at my feet
Rested a silent sea of hoary mist.   20

A hundred hills their dusky backs upheaved
All over this still ocean; and beyond,
Far, far beyond, the solid vapours stretched,
In headlands, tongues, and promontory shapes,
Into the main Atlantic, that appeared 25
To dwindle, and give up his majesty,
Usurped upon far as the sight could reach.
Not so the ethereal vault; encroachment none
Was there, nor loss; only the inferior stars
Had disappeared, or shed a fainter light 30
In the clear presence of the full-orbed Moon,
Who, from her sovereign elevation, gazed
Upon the billowy ocean, as it lay
All meek and silent, save that through a rift—
Not distant from the shore on which we stood, 35
A fixed, abysmal, gloomy, breathing-place—
Mounted the roar of waters, torrents, streams
Innumerable, roaring with one voice!
Heard over earth and sea, and, in that hour,
For so it seemed, felt by the starry heavens. 40

WORDSWORTH

1. Which of these pictures do you like best?

2. Can you add any Moon Pictures from the poems you have already read?

Notes: page 190.

THE RAIDERS

Last night a wind from Lammermoor came roaring up the glen
With the tramp of trooping horses and the laugh of reckless men,
And struck a mailed hand on the gate and cried in rebel glee:
"Come forth, come forth, my Borderer, and ride the March with me!"

I said "Oh Wind of Lammermoor, the night's too dark to ride,
And all the men that fill the glen are ghosts of men that died!
The floods are down in Bowmont Burn, the moss is fetlock-deep;
Go back, wild Wind of Lammermoor, to Lauderdale—and sleep!"

Out spoke the Wind of Lammermoor, "We know the road right well,
The road that runs by Kale and Jed across the Carter Fell,
There is no man of all the men in this grey troop of mine
But blind might ride the Border side from Teviothead to Tyne!"

The horses fretted on their bits and pawed the flints to fire,
The riders swung them to the south full-faced to their desire;
"Come!" said the Wind of Lammermoor, and spoke full scornfully,
"Have ye no pride to mount and ride your father's road with me?"

A roan horse to the gate they led, foam-flecked and
  travelled far,
A snorting roan that tossed his head and flashed his
  forehead star;
There came a sound of clashing steel and hoof-tramp
  up the glen,
And two by two we cantered through, a troop of
  ghostly men!   20
  * * * * *

I know not if the farms we fired are burned to ashes
  yet!
I know not if the stirks grew tired before the stars were
  set!
I only know that late last night when northern winds
  blew free,
A troop of men rode up the glen and brought a horse
  for me!

WILL H. OGILVIE
(20th Century)

1. A poem full of sound:
   - (a) Note how the rhythm helps to bring it out.
   - (b) Note the internal rhyming, as in the last stanza, lines 21-22, " fired ", " tired "; line 24, " men ", " glen ".
   - (c) Note the alliteration, as in line 2, " tramp ", " trooping "; line 10, " road ", " runs ".
   - (d) Note the words that suggest sound, as in line 1, " roaring "; line 19, " clashing ".

   There are many more examples of (b), (c) and (d).

2. Stanza 3. Compare this with the passage from Scott on the next page.

3. Are the last two lines true?

4. If the first line ran
   I dreamt a wind from Lammermoor came roaring up the glen,
   what would be the effect on the poem?

5. How would you read the poem?

6. What is the atmosphere of the poem, and in which stanza do you feel it most?

   Notes: page 190.

SIR WILLIAM OF DELORAINE, GOOD AT NEED

A stark moss-trooping Scot was he,
As e'er couched Border lance by knee;
Through Solway sands, through Tarras Moss,
Blindfold, he knew the paths to cross;
By wily turns, by desperate bounds, 5
Had baffled Percy's best blood-hounds;
In Eske, or Liddel, fords were none,
But he would ride them one by one;
Alike to him was time or tide,
December's snow, or July's pride; 10
Alike to him was tide or time,
Moonless midnight, or matin prime:
Steady of heart, and stout of hand,
As ever drove prey from Cumberland;
Five times outlawed had he been, 15
By England's King, and Scotland's Queen.

"The Lay of The Last Minstrel", *Canto I, Stanza* 21.

SCOTT
(1771-1832)

THE FORAY

The last of our steers on the board has been spread,
And the last flask of wine in our goblet is red;
Up, up, my brave kinsmen! belt swords and begone,
There are dangers to dare, and there's spoil to be won.

The eyes, that so lately mix'd glances with ours, 5
For a space must be dim, as they gaze from the towers,
And strive to distinguish through tempest and gloom
The prance of the steed and the toss of the plume.

The rain is descending; the wind rises loud;
And the moon her red beacon has veil'd with a cloud; 10
'Tis the better, my mates! for the warder's dull eye
Shall in confidence slumber, nor dream we are nigh.

Our steeds are impatient! I hear my blithe Grey!
There is life in his hoof-clang, and hope in his neigh;
Like the flash of a meteor, the glance of his mane 15
Shall marshal your march through the darkness and rain.

The drawbridge has dropp'd, the bugle has blown;
One pledge is to quaff yet—then mount and begone!—
To their honour and peace, that shall rest with the slain;
To their health and their glee, that see Teviot again! 20

SCOTT
(1771-1832)

1. What is the difference between the atmosphere of this poem and that of "The Raiders" (page 118)?
2. Compare stanza 3 of this poem with stanza 3 of "The Raiders".
3. Compare stanza 4 of this poem with stanza 5 of "The Raiders".
4. Compare stanza 5 of this poem with stanza 6 of "The Raiders".
5. Which poem do you prefer?
   Notes: page 190.

THE WAR SONG OF DINAS VAWR

The mountain sheep are sweeter,
But the valley sheep are fatter;
We therefore deemed it meeter
To carry off the latter.
We made an expedition;   5
We met a host, and quelled it;
We forced a strong position,
And killed the men who held it.

On Dyfed's richest valley,
Where herds of kine were browsing,   10
We made a mighty sally,
To furnish our carousing.
Fierce warriors rushed to meet us;
We met them, and o'erthrew them;
They struggled hard to beat us;   15
But we conquered them, and slew them.

As we drove our prize at leisure,
The king marched forth to catch us:
His rage surpassed all measure,
But his people could not match us.   20
He fled to his hall-pillars;
And, ere our force we led off,
Some sacked his house and cellars,
While others cut his head off.

We there, in strife bewild'ring,   25
Spilt blood enough to swim in;
We orphaned many children,
And widowed many women.
The eagles and the ravens
We glutted with our foemen;   30
The heroes and the cravens,
The spearmen and the bowmen.

We brought away from battle,
And much their land bemoaned them,
Two thousand head of cattle,   35
And the head of him who owned them:
Ednyfed, King of Dyfed,
His head was borne before us;
His wine and beasts supplied our feasts,
And his overthrow, our chorus.   40

PEACOCK
(1785-1866)

1. Compare the atmosphere of this poem with that of "The Raiders" and "The Foray".

2. The rhymes are all double.

   The mountain sheep are sweet,
   But the valley sheep are fat.

   How do you like it thus?

3. Sometimes the double rhyme gives a touch of dry humour to the line.

4. When you read this poem aloud do you give two or three beats to the line?

5. What is peculiar in lines 37 and 39?

   Notes: page 191.

MACPHERSON'S FAREWELL

Farewell, ye dungeons dark and strong,
  The wretch's destinie :
Macpherson's time will not be long
  On yonder gallows tree.

    Sae rantingly, sae wantonly,
      Sae dauntingly gaed he;
    He play'd a spring and danc'd it round
      Below the gallows tree.

Oh, what is death but parting breath?
  On mony a bloody plain
I've dar'd his face, and in this place
  I scorn him yet again !

Untie these bands from off my hands
  And bring to me my sword !
And there's no a man in all Scotland
  But I'll brave him at a word.

I've liv'd a life of sturt and strife;
  I die by treacherie :
It burns my heart I must depart
  And not avenged be.

Now farewell light, thou sunshine bright;
  And all beneath the sky !
May coward shame distain his name,
  The wretch that dares not die !

  Sae rantingly, sae wantonly,
    Sae dauntingly gaed he,
  He play'd a spring and danc'd it round
    Below the gallows tree.

BURNS
(1759-1796)

rantingly: *cheerfully*   spring: *cheerful tune*
wantonly: *carelessly*   sturt: *violence*
dauntingly: *defiantly*

The freebooter, Macpherson, terrorised the shires of Aberdeen, Moray, and Banff in the second half of the seventeenth century. Captured at length, and sentenced to death, he passed the time in his dungeon composing the words and music of a song on his own life story. Burns' verses were based on Macpherson's, and written to his air.

1. Which of the last three poems does this resemble in spirit ? Does Macpherson strike you as one of the Raiders, or riding in the Foray, or following Dinas Vawr ?

2. Of which poem earlier in this book is this one a real illustration ?

Notes: page 191.

PIBROCH OF DONUIL DHU

Pibroch of Donuil Dhu,
  Pibroch of Donuil,
Wake thy wild voice anew,
  Summon Clan-Conuil.
Come away, come away,   5
  Hark to the summons!
Come in your war array,
  Gentles and commons.

Come from deep glen and
  From mountain so rocky,   10
The war-pipe and pennon
  Are at Inverlochy.
Come every hill-plaid and
  True heart that wears one,
Come every steel blade and   15
  Strong hand that bears one.

Leave untended the herd,
  The flock without shelter;
Leave the corpse uninterr'd,
  The bride at the altar;   20
Leave the deer, leave the steer,
  Leave nets and barges:
Come with your fighting gear,
  Broadswords and targes.

Come as the winds come, when
   Forests are rended,
Come as the waves come, when
   Navies are stranded :
Faster come, faster come,
   Faster and faster,
Chief, vassal, page, and groom,
   Tenant and master.

Fast they come, fast they come,
   See how they gather!
Wide waves the eagle plume
   Blended with heather.
Cast your plaids, draw your blades,
   Forward each man set!
Pibroch of Donuil Dhu
   Knell for the onset!

SCOTT
(1771-1832)

This poem is supposed to refer to the expedition made by Donald Balloch in 1431. With a force from the Hebrides he attacked Lochaber and defeated the Earls of Mar and Caithness at Inverlochy.

1. This is a poem you want to read fast. Which stanza goes fastest?
2. One stanza definitely starts more slowly. Find it and compare the metre with that of one of the fast stanzas.
3. Note the last line. What would be the effect if we substituted " sound " for " knell " ? Compare with this Byron's description of the sound of the pipes at Waterloo:

> *And wild and high the ' Camerons' Gathering ' rose :*
> *The war-note of Lochiel, which Albyn's hills*
> *Have heard, and heard, too, have her Saxon foes :*
> *How in the noon of night that pibroch thrills*
> *Savage and shrill !*

Notes: page 191.

HARLAW

Now haud your tongue, baith wife and carle,
   And listen, great and sma',
And I will sing of Glenallan's Earl
   That fought on the red Harlaw.

The cronach's cried on Bennachie,
   And doun the Don and a',
And Hieland and Lawland may mournfu' be
   For the sair field of Harlaw.

They saddled a hundred milk-white steeds,
   They hae bridled a hundred black,
With a chafron of steel on each horse's head,
   And a good knight upon his back.

They hadna ridden a mile, a mile,
   A mile, but barely ten,
When Donald came branking down the brae
   Wi' twenty thousand men.

Their tartans they were waving wide.
   Their glaives were glancing clear,
The pibrochs rang frae side to side,
   Would deafen ye to hear.

The great Earl in his stirrups stood
   That Highland host to see:
" Now here a knight that's stout and good
   May prove a jeopardie:

" What wouldst thou do, my squire so gay,
   That rides beside my reyne,
Were ye Glenallan's Earl the day,
   And I were Roland Cheyne?

"To turn the rein were sin and shame,
  To fight were wond'rous peril,   30
What would ye do now, Roland Cheyne,
  Were ye Glenallan's Earl?"

"Were I Glenallan's Earl this tide,
  And ye were Roland Cheyne,
The spur should be in my horse's side,   35
  And the bridle upon his mane.

"If they hae twenty thousand blades,
  And we twice ten times ten,
Yet they hae but their tartan plaids,
  And we are mail-clad men.   40

"My horse shall ride through ranks sae rude
  As through the moorland fern,
Then ne'er let the gentle Norman blude
  Grow cauld for Highland kerne."

SCOTT
(1771-1832)

haud: *hold*
carle: *man*
cronach: *coronach, dirge*
chafron: *plate to protect face of horse*

branking: *swaggering*
glaives: *Highland bills*
kerne: *rabble footmen*

1. In Scott's novel "The Antiquary", an old woman, Elspeth, sings this as an old ballad. In how many ways does it resemble an old ballad?

2. Compare lines 5 and 19. What word in each line gives the difference between the Coronach and the Pibroch? See "Coronach" in Book II, and "Pibroch of Donuil Dhu" in this book (page 126).

3. This poem is a fragment, and there is no description of the battle, yet we know the result. Where do we find this?

Notes: page 192.

THE VISION OF BELSHAZZAR

The King was on his throne,
   The Satraps throng'd the hall:
A thousand bright lamps shone
   O'er that high festival.
A thousand cups of gold,   5
   In Judah deem'd divine—
Jehovah's vessels hold
   The godless Heathen's wine.

In that same hour and hall,
   The fingers of a hand   10
Came forth against the wall
   And wrote as if on sand:
The fingers of a man;
   A solitary hand
Along the letters ran,   15
   And traced them like a wand.

The monarch saw, and shook,
   And bade no more rejoice;
All bloodless wax'd his look,
   And tremulous his voice.   20
"Let the men of lore appear,
   The wisest of the earth,
And expound the words of fear
   Which mar our royal mirth."

Chaldea's seers are good,   25
   But here they have no skill;
And the unknown letters stood
   Untold and awful still.
And Babel's men of age
   Are wise and deep in lore;   30
But now they were not sage,
   They saw—but knew no more.

A captive in the land,
  A stranger and a youth,
He heard the king's command,
  He saw the writing's truth.
The lamps around were bright,
  The prophecy in view;
He read it on that night,
  The morrow proved it true.

"Belshazzar's grave is made,
  His kingdom pass'd away,
He, in the balance weigh'd,
  Is light and worthless clay;
The shroud his robe of state,
  His canopy the stone;
The Mede is at his gate!
  The Persian on his throne!"

BYRON
(1788-1824)

1. Read the story in the Bible—Daniel, Ch. V. What in the story attracted Byron and made him want to write this poem?

2. Note the things he has omitted. Can you tell why he omits them?

3. The poem is practically a series of pictures. Give a name to each.

4. Should this poem be read quickly or slowly?

Notes: page 192.

DAVID'S LAMENT FOR JONATHAN

The beauty of Israel is slain upon thy high places:
how are the mighty fallen!
Tell it not in Gath, publish it not in the streets of
Askelon; lest the daughters of the Philistines
rejoice, lest the daughters of the uncircumcised
triumph.
Ye mountains of Gilboa, let there be no dew, neither
let there be rain upon you, nor fields of offerings:
for there the shield of the mighty is vilely cast
away, the shield of Saul, as though he had not been
anointed with oil.
From the blood of the slain, from the fat of the mighty,
the bow of Jonathan turned not back, and the sword
of Saul returned not empty.
Saul and Jonathan were lovely and pleasant in their
lives, and in their death they were not divided:
they were swifter than eagles, they were stronger
than lions.
Ye daughters of Israel, weep over Saul, who clothed
you in scarlet, with other delights, who put on
ornaments of gold upon your apparel.
How are the mighty fallen in the midst of the battle!
O Jonathan, thou wast slain in thine high places.
I am distressed for thee, my brother Jonathan: very
pleasant hast thou been unto me: thy love to me
was wonderful, passing the love of women.
How are the mighty fallen, and the weapons of war
perished!

II SAMUEL, I., 19-27.

1. The last poem was based on a passage from the Bible.
   The above is a passage taken directly from the Bible.
   Is it poetry or prose?
2. What is the most poetical, the most striking thing in
   this passage?
   Notes: page 193.

INCIDENT OF THE FRENCH CAMP

I

You know, we French stormed Ratisbon:
  A mile or so away,
On a little mound, Napoleon
  Stood on our storming-day;
With neck out-thrust, you fancy how, 5
Legs wide, arms locked behind,
As if to balance the prone brow
  Oppressive with its mind.

II

Just as perhaps he mused, " My plans
  That soar, to earth may fall, 10
Let once my army-leader Lannes
Waver at yonder wall "—
Out 'twixt the battery-smokes there flew
  A rider, bound on bound
Full-galloping; nor bridle drew 15
  Until he reached the mound.

III

Then off there flung in smiling joy,
  And held himself erect
By just his horse's mane, a boy:
  You hardly could suspect— 20
(So tight he kept his lips compressed,
  Scarce any blood came through)
You looked twice ere you saw his breast
  Was all but shot in two.

IV

"Well," cried he, "Emperor, by God's grace   25
  We've got you Ratisbon!
The Marshal's in the market-place,
  And you'll be there anon
To see your flag-bird flap his vans
  Where I, to heart's desire,   30
Perched him!" The chief's eye flashed; his plans
  Soared up again like fire.

V

The chief's eye flashed; but presently
  Softened itself, as sheathes
A film the mother-eagle's eye   35
  When her bruised eaglet breathes;
"You're wounded!" "Nay," the soldier's pride
  Touched to the quick, he said:
"I'm killed, Sire!" And his chief beside
  Smiling the boy fell dead.   40

BROWNING
(1812-1889)

1. Note the picture of Napoleon in stanza I.

2. Stanza II. Why is the boy in such haste?

3. The boy is wounded to death, yet he seems entirely happy. What reasons can you give for his happiness?

4. Is there anything specially appropriate in comparing Napoleon to the mother-eagle and the boy to the eaglet?

5. Is this a sad poem?

6. Note the variations in speed. Where does the poem go fastest and what lines are particularly slow?

Notes: page 193.

BOOT AND SADDLE

Boot, saddle, to horse, and away!
Rescue my castle before the hot day
Brightens to blue from its silvery grey,
    Boot, saddle, to horse, and away!

Ride past the suburbs, asleep as you'd say;   5
Many's the friend there, will listen and pray
" God's luck to gallants that strike up the lay—
    Boot, saddle, to horse, and away!"

Forty miles off, like a roebuck at bay,
Flouts Castle Brancepeth the Roundheads' array: 10
Who laughs, " Good fellows ere this, by my fay,
    Boot, saddle, to horse, and away!"

Who? My wife Gertrude; that, honest and gay,
Laughs when you talk of surrendering, " Nay!
I've better counsellors; what counsel they?   15
    Boot, saddle, to horse, and away!"

BROWNING
(1812-1889)

1. This is one of Browning's "Cavalier Tunes". They have all a fine swinging rhythm. Note the unchanging rhyme. Here is a stanza from another:
    > *Kentish Sir Byng stood for his King:*
    > *Bidding the crop-headed Parliament swing;*
    > *And, pressing a troop unable to stoop*
    > *And see the rogues flourish and honest folk droop,*
    > *Marched them along, fifty score strong,*
    > *Great-hearted gentlemen, singing this song.*

2. Compare the rhythm of " Boot and Saddle " with that of " Kentish Sir Byng " and also that of " The Highwayman ", page 108, and " How They Brought the Good News " in Book II. Arrange these four poems in order of speed.

Notes: page 193.

WILL YE NO COME BACK AGAIN?

Will ye no come back again?
Will ye no come back again?
Better lo'ed ye canna be,
Will ye no come back again?

Bonnie Charlie's now awa',　　　　　　　　　5
　Safely owre the friendly main;
Mony a heart will break in twa,
　Should he ne'er come back again.

Ye trusted in your Hieland men,
　They trusted you, dear Charlie;　　　　　10
They kent you hiding in the glen,
　Your cleadin' was but barely.

English bribes were a' in vain;
　An' e'en though puirer we may be,
Siller canna buy the heart　　　　　　　　15
　That beats aye for thine and thee.

We watched thee in the gloaming hour,
　We watched thee in the morning grey;
Though thirty thousand pounds they'd gie,
　Oh there is nane that wad betray.　　　20

Sweet's the laverock's note and lang,
　Lilting wildly up the glen;
But aye to me he sings ae sang,
　Will ye no come back again?　　LADY NAIRNE
　　　　　　　　　　　　　　　　(1766-1845)

kent: *knew*　　　　　　　cleadin': *clothing*

1. Stanza 1. This is one of the best known stanzas in Scottish poetry. Why do you think it has become so popular?
2. In stanza 1, lines 1, 2 and 4 are exactly the same. What would be the effect of omitting the first two lines? Compare this stanza with the first stanza of "Open the Door to Me, Oh!" page 104.
3. A proof of the popularity of stanza 1 is that most people know not only the words but the music.
Notes: page 194.

BONNIE PRINCE CHARLIE

Follow thee! follow thee! wha wadna follow thee?
Lang hast thou loved and trusted us fairly!
Charlie, Charlie, wha wadna follow thee,
King o' the Highland hearts, bonnie Prince Charlie?

Cam ye by Athol, lad wi' the philabeg, 5
Down by the Tummel, or banks o' the Garry;
Saw ye our lads, wi' their bonnets and white cockades,
Leaving their mountains to follow Prince Charlie?

I hae but ae son, my gallant young Donald;
But if I had ten, they should follow Glengarry. 10
Health to M'Donnell, and gallant Clan-Ronald,
For these are the men that will die for their Charlie.

I'll to Lochiel, and Appin, and kneel to them,
Down by Lord Murray, and Roy of Kildarlie;
Brave M'Intosh, he shall fly to the field with them; 15
These are the lads I can trust wi' my Charlie!

Down through the Lowlands, down wi' the Whigamore!
Loyal true Highlanders, down wi' them rarely!
Ronald and Donald, drive on wi' the broad claymore,
Over the necks of the foes of Prince Charlie! 20

HOGG
(1770-1835)

1. "Boot and Saddle" and "Kentish Sir Byng" are both Cavalier songs. This poem and the last are both Jacobite songs. What is the difference in feeling between the two groups? Are there any other differences between them?

Notes: page 194.

HOME THOUGHTS FROM THE SEA

Nobly, nobly Cape Saint Vincent to the North-west
   died away;
Sunset ran, one glorious blood-red, reeking into Cadiz
   Bay;
Bluish 'mid the burning water, full in face Trafalgar
   lay;
In the dimmest North-east distance dawned Gibraltar
   grand and grey;
" Here and here did England help me: how can I
   help England?"—say,   5
Whoso turns as I, this evening, turn to God to praise
   and pray,
While Jove's planet rises yonder, silent over Africa.

                            BROWNING
                           (1812-1889)

1. Lines 1-4. This is not Geography, but Poetry. Why then all these names and directions?

2. Line 5. This is the key to the poem. If you understand this line you should understand the whole poem.

Notes: page 194.

A BALLAD OF CAPE ST. VINCENT

Now, Bill, ain't it prime to be a-sailin',
   Slippin' easy, splashin' up the sea,
Dossin' snug aneath the weather-railin',
   Quiddin' bonded Jacky out a-lee?
English sea astern us and afore us,   5
   Reaching out three thousand miles ahead,
God's own stars a-risin' solemn o'er us,
   And—yonder's Cape St. Vincent and the Dead.

There they lie, Bill, man and mate together,
   Dreamin' out the dog-watch down below,   10
Anchored in the Port of Pleasant Weather,
   Waiting for the Bo'sun's call to blow.
Over them the tide goes lappin', swayin',
   Under them's the wide bay's muddy bed,
And it's pleasant dreams—to them—to hear us sayin', 15
   Yonder's Cape St. Vincent and the Dead.

Hear that P. and O. boat's engines dronin',
   Beating out of time and out of tune,
Ripping past with every plate a-groanin',
   Spitting smoke and cinders at the moon?   20
Ports a-lit like little stars a-settin',
   See 'em glintin' yaller, green, and red,
Loggin' twenty knots, Bill—but forgettin',
   Yonder's Cape St. Vincent and the Dead.

They're " discharged " now, Billy, " left the service," 25
  Rough an' bitter was the watch they stood,
Drake an' Blake, an' Collingwood an' Jervis,
  Nelson, Rodney, Hawke, an' Howe an' Hood.
They 'd a hard time, haulin' an' directin';
  There's the flag they left us, Billy—tread 30
Straight an' keep it flyin'—recollectin',
  Yonder's Cape St. Vincent and the Dead.

JOHN MASEFIELD
(20th Century)

Quiddin' bonded Jacky: *Chewing negro-head tobacco.*

1. Line 5. What is the meaning of this line?

2. Lines 23-24. What are they forgetting?

3. Read the question in line 5 of the last poem. Can you find an answer to it in this poem?

4. If we had to omit one stanza of this poem I think it would be the third. Read the poem, omitting it, and you will see why.

Notes: page 194.

HOW SLEEP THE BRAVE

How sleep the brave who sink to rest,
By all their country's wishes blest!
When Spring, with dewy fingers cold,
Returns to deck their hallowed mould,
She there shall dress a sweeter sod   5
Than Fancy's feet have ever trod.

By fairy hands their knell is rung;
By forms unseen their dirge is sung;
There Honour comes, a pilgrim grey,
To bless the turf that wraps their clay;   10
And Freedom shall awhile repair,
To dwell, a weeping hermit, there!

COLLINS
(1721-1759)

1. Stanza 2. Montégut claims that since Ariel's "Full Fathom Five" (1612) nothing had appeared comparable in its kind to the elfin music of this stanza written in 1746.

2. The following stanza is from a modern poem, "For The Fallen", by Laurence Binyon:

> *They shall grow not old, as we that are left grow old :*
> *Age shall not weary them, nor the years condemn.*
> *At the going down of the sun and in the morning*
> *We will remember them.*

The tone of this stanza is quite different from that of "How Sleep the Brave". Can you account for the difference?

Notes: page 195.

THE REVENGE

A BALLAD OF THE FLEET

I

At Flores in the Azores Sir Richard Grenville lay,
And a pinnace, like a flutter'd bird, came flying from far away:
"Spanish ships of war at sea! we have sighted fifty-three!"
Then sware Lord Thomas Howard: "'Fore God I am no coward;
But I cannot meet them here, for my ships are out of gear, 5
And the half my men are sick. I must fly, but follow quick.
We are six ships of the line; can we fight with fifty-three?"

II

Then spake Sir Richard Grenville: "I know you are no coward;
You fly them for a moment to fight with them again.
But I've ninety men and more that are lying sick ashore. 10
I should count myself the coward if I left them, my Lord Howard,
To these Inquisition dogs and the devildoms of Spain."

III

So Lord Howard past away with five ships of war that day,
Till he melted like a cloud in the silent summer heaven;
But Sir Richard bore in hand all his sick men from the land 15
Very carefully and slow,
Men of Bideford in Devon.

And we laid them on the ballast down below;
For we brought them all aboard,
And they blest him in their pain, that they were not left 20
  to Spain,
To the thumbscrew and the stake, for the glory of the
  Lord.

IV

He had only a hundred seamen to work the ship and to
  fight,
And he sailed away from Flores till the Spaniard came
  in sight,
With his huge sea-castles heaving upon the weather bow.
" Shall we fight or shall we fly? 25
Good Sir Richard, tell us now,
For to fight is but to die!
There'll be little of us left by the time this sun be set."
And Sir Richard said again: "We be all good English men.
Let us bang these dogs of Seville, the children of the devil, 30
For I never turn'd my back upon Don or devil yet."

V

Sir Richard spoke and he laugh'd, and we roar'd a
  hurrah, and so
The little *Revenge* ran on, sheer into the heart of the foe,
With her hundred fighters on deck, and her ninety sick
  below;
For half of their fleet to the right and half to the left were 35
  seen,
And the little *Revenge* ran on thro' the long sea-lane
  between.

VI

Thousands of their soldiers look'd down from their decks and laugh'd,
Thousands of their seamen made mock at the mad little craft
Running on and on, till delay'd
By their mountain-like *San Philip* that, of fifteen hundred tons, 40
And up-shadowing high above us with her yawning tiers of guns,
Took the breath from our sails, and we stay'd.

VII

And while now the great *San Philip* hung above us like a cloud
Whence the thunderbolt will fall
Long and loud,
Four galleons drew away 45
From the Spanish fleet that day,
And two upon the larboard and two upon the starboard lay,
And the battle-thunder broke from them all.

VIII

But anon the great *San Philip*, she bethought herself and went 50
Having that within her womb that had left her ill content;
And the rest they came aboard us, and they fought us hand to hand,
For a dozen times they came with their pikes and musqueteers,
And a dozen times we shook 'em off as a dog that shakes his ears
When he leaps from the water to the land. 55

IX

And the sun went down, and the stars came out far
  over the summer sea,
But never a moment ceased the fight of the one and
  the fifty-three.
Ship after ship, the whole night long, their high-built
  galleons came,
Ship after ship, the whole night long, with her battle-
  thunder and flame;
Ship after ship, the whole night long, drew back with   60
  her dead and her shame.
For some were sunk and many were shatter'd, and so
  could fight us no more—
God of battles, was ever a battle like this in the world
  before?

X

For he said "Fight on! fight on!"
Tho' his vessel was all but a wreck;
And it chanced that, when half of the short summer   65
  night was gone,
With a grisly wound to be drest he had left the deck,
But a bullet struck him that was dressing it suddenly
  dead,
And himself he was wounded again in the side and the
  head,
And he said "Fight on! fight on!"

XI

And the night went down, and the sun smiled out far   70
  over the summer sea,
And the Spanish fleet with broken sides lay round us all
  in a ring;

But they dared not touch us again, for they fear'd that we still could sting,
So they watch'd what the end would be.
And we had not fought them in vain,
But in perilous plight were we, 75
Seeing forty of our poor hundred were slain,
And half of the rest of us maim'd for life
In the crash of the cannonades and the desperate strife;
And the sick men down in the hold were most of them stark and cold,
And the pikes were all broken or bent, and the powder was all of it spent; 80
And the masts and the rigging were lying over the side;
But Sir Richard cried in his English pride,
"We have fought such a fight for a day and a night
As may never be fought again!
We have won great glory, my men! 85
And a day less or more
At sea or ashore,
We die—does it matter when?
Sink me the ship, Master Gunner—sink her, split her in twain!
Fall into the hands of God, not into the hands of Spain!" 90

XII

And the gunner said, "Ay, ay," but the seamen made reply:
"We have children, we have wives,
And the Lord hath spared our lives.
We will make the Spaniard promise, if we yield, to let us go;
We shall live to fight again, and to strike another blow." 95
And the lion there lay dying, and they yielded to the foe.

XIII

And the stately Spanish men to their flagship bore him then,
Where they laid him by the mast, old Sir Richard caught at last,
And they praised him to his face with their courtly foreign grace;
But he rose upon their decks, and he cried: 100
" I have fought for Queen and Faith like a valiant man and true;
I have only done my duty as a man is bound to do:
With a joyful spirit I Sir Richard Grenville die!"
And he fell upon their decks and he died.

XIV

And they stared at the dead that had been so valiant 105 and true,
And had holden the power and glory of Spain so cheap
That he dared her with one little ship and his English few;
Was he devil or man? He was devil for aught they knew,
But they sank his body with honour down into the deep,
And they mann'd the *Revenge* with a swarthier alien 110 crew,
And away she sail'd with her loss and long'd for her own;
When a wind from the lands they had ruin'd awoke from sleep,
And the water began to heave and the weather to moan,
And or ever that evening ended a great gale blew,
And a wave like the wave that is raised by an earthquake 115 grew,

Till it smote on their hulls and their sails and their masts and their flags,
And the whole sea plunged and fell on the shot-shatter'd navy of Spain,
And the little *Revenge* herself went down by the island crags
To be lost evermore in the main.

TENNYSON
(1809-1892)

1. This great fight was fought in 1592. The story was first told by Sir Walter Raleigh in Hakluyt's "Voyages". In the following pages I give extracts from the "Voyages", so that Tennyson's poetry may be compared with the original.
2. Stanzas I-III. Was Lord Thomas Howard right to fly from the enemy and leave Grenville?
3. Stanza III. Which is the most beautiful line in this stanza?
4. Stanza IV. Compare this with lines 7-17, prose. Which gives the better picture?
5. Stanzas V and VI. Compare this with lines 17-30, prose. What do we lose in the verse?
6. Stanza VIII, lines 1-2. Compare with lines 32-35, prose. Which do you prefer?
7. Which are the most beautiful lines in stanza VIII?
8. Lines 38-43, prose. This, which shows the fine spirit of Grenville, is omitted from the verse.
9. Stanzas IX and X. Compare with lines 44-61, prose. Note that the fine incident in lines 56-61, prose, is not touched on in the verse.
10. Stanza XI. Compare with lines 62-80, prose. Which gives the better picture of the desperate state of the *Revenge*?
11. Stanza XIII. Compare this with lines 81-89, prose. Which do you prefer?
12. Stanza XIV. Which are the most beautiful lines in this stanza?
13. The rhyme and the rhythm are very interesting. Draw up a rhyme scheme for stanza I. You will find lines of 2, 3, 4, 5, 6, and 7 beats in stanza XI.

Notes: Page 195.

A Report of the trueth of the fight about the Isles of Açores, the last of August 1591, *betwixt the* Revenge, *one of her Majesties Shippes, and an Armada of the King of Spaine; Penned by the honourable Sir Walter Ralegh knight.*

... The Spanish fleet having shrouded their approach by reason of the Island; were now so soone at hand, as our shippes had scarce time to way their anchors, but some of them were driven to let slippe their Cables and set saile. Sir Richard Grinvile was the last that wayed, to recover the men that were upon the Island, which otherwise had bene lost. The L. Thomas with the rest very hardly recovered the winde, which Sir Richard Grinvile not being able to doe, was perswaded by the Master and others to cut his maine sayle,* and cast about, and to trust to the sayling of the ship; for the squadron of Sivil were on his weather bow. But Sir Richard utterly refused to turne from the enemie, alleaging that hee would rather choose to die, then to dishonour himselfe, his countrey, and her Majesties shippe, perswading his companie that hee would passe through the two squadrons, in despight of them, and enforce those of Sivil to give him way. Which hee performed upon divers of the formost, who, as the Mariners terme it, sprang their luffe, and fell under the lee of the *Revenge*. But the other course had beene the better, and might right well have bene answered in so great an impossibility of prevaling. Notwithstanding out of the greatnesse of his minde, he could not be perswaded. In the meane while as hee attended those which were nearest him, the great *San Philip* being in the winde of him, and comming towards him, becalmed his sailes in such sort, as the shippe could neither make way, nor feele the helme: so huge and

---

* "To cut his maine sayle" meant to cut the gaskets and let it **fall**, *i.e.* to set the sail.

high carged was the Spanish ship, being of a thousand
and five hundreth tuns.   Who after layd the *Revenge*
aboord.

* * * * * *

But the great *San Philip* having received the lower
tire of the *Revenge*, discharged with crossebar-shot,
shifted herselfe with all diligence from her sides, utterly
misliking her first entertainement. Some say that the
shippe foundred, but we cannot report it for truth,
unlesse we were assured.

* * * * * *

In the beginning of the fight, the *George Noble* of
London having received some shot thorow her by the
Armadas, fell under the lee of the *Revenge*, and asked
Sir Richard what he would command him, being but
one of the victuallers and of small force: Sir Richard
bid him save himselfe, and leave him to his fortune.

* * * * * *

But to returne to the fight, the Spanish ships which
attempted to bord the *Revenge*, as they were wounded and
beaten off, so always others came in their places, she
having never lesse then two mighty Gallions by her sides,
and aboard her: So that ere the morning, from three
of the clocke the day before, there had fifteene severall
Armadas assayled her; and all so ill approved their
entertainement, as they were by the breake of day, far
more willing to harken to a composition, then hastily to
make any more assaults or entries. But as the day
encreased, so our men decreased: and as the light
grew more and more, by so much more grewe our
discomforts. For none appeared in sight but enemies,
saving one small ship called the *Pilgrim*, commaunded
by Jacob Whiddon, who hovered all night to see the
successe : but in the morning bearing with the *Revenge*,
was hunted like a hare amongst many ravenous houndes,
but escaped.

* * * * * *

All the powder of the *Revenge* to the last barrell was
now spent, all her pikes broken, fortie of her best men
slaine, and the most part of the rest hurt. In the
beginning of the fight shee had but one hundreth free
from sicknes, and fourscore & ten sicke, laid in hold
upon the Ballast. A small troup to man such a ship,
& a weake garrison to resist so mighty an army. By those
hundred al was susteined, the voleis, boordings, and
entrings of fifteen ships of warre, besides those which
beat her at large. On the contrary, the Spanish were
always supplied with souldiers brought from every
squadron : all maner of Armes and powder at will.
Unto ours there remained no comfort at all, no hope,
no supply either of ships, men, or weapons; the Mastes
all beaten over boord, all her tackle cut asunder, her
upper worke altogether rased, and in effect evened shee
was with the water, but the very foundation or bottome
of a ship, nothing being left over head either for flight
or defence.

*   *   *   *   *   *

Sir Richard died as it is sayd, the second or third
day aboord the Generall, and was by them greatly
bewailed. What became of his body, whether it were
buried in the sea or on the land we know not : the
comfort that remayneth to his friends is, that hee hath
ended his life honourably in respect of the reputation
wonne to his nation and countrey, and of the same to his
posteritie, and that being dead, he hath not outlived
his owne honour.

*   *   *   *   *   *

If all the rest had entred, all had bene lost : for the
very hugenes of the Spanish fleete, if no other violence
had beene offered, would have crusht them betweene them
into shivers. Of which the dishonour and losse to the
Queene had bene farre greater then the spoyle or harme
that the enemie could any way have received.

RALEIGH
(1552-1618)

THE GOLDEN CITY OF ST. MARY

Out beyond the sunset, could I but find the way,
Is a sleepy blue laguna which widens to a bay,
And there's the Blessed City—so the sailors say—
    The Golden City of St. Mary.

It's built of fair marble—white—without a stain,   5
And in the cool twilight when the sea-winds wane
The bells chime faintly, like a soft, warm rain,
    In the Golden City of St. Mary.

Among the green palm-trees where the fire-flies shine,
Are the white tavern tables where the gallants dine, 10
Singing slow Spanish songs like old mulled wine,
    In the Golden City of St. Mary.

Oh I'll be shipping sunset-wards and westward-ho
Through the green toppling combers a-shattering into
  snow,
Till I come to quiet moorings and a watch below, 15
    In the Golden City of St. Mary.

                            JOHN MASEFIELD
                               (*20th Century*)

1. See lines 5, 9 and 10. Why is it called the *Golden* city of St. Mary?

2. Line 11. The following lines are from Masefield's poem, " Beauty " :

    I have seen dawn and sunset on moors and windy hills

    Coming in solemn beauty like slow old tunes of Spain.

3. On the next page are printed the first three stanzas of Longfellow's " My Lost Youth ". In what way do the two poems resemble each other?

Notes: page 196.

MY LOST YOUTH

Often I think of the beautiful town
  That is seated by the sea;
Often in thought go up and down
The pleasant streets of that dear old town,
  And my youth comes back to me.
  And a verse of a Lapland song
  Is haunting my memory still:
  " A boy's will is the wind's will,
And the thoughts of youth are long, long thoughts."

I can see the shadowy lines of its trees,
  And catch, in sudden gleams,
The sheen of the far-surrounding seas,
And islands that were the Hesperides
  Of all my boyish dreams.
  And the burden of that old song,
  It murmurs and whispers still:
  " A boy's will is the wind's will,
And the thoughts of youth are long, long thoughts."

I remember the black wharves and the slips,
  And the sea-tides tossing free;
And Spanish sailors with bearded lips,
And the beauty and mystery of the ships,
  And the magic of the sea.
  And the voice of that wayward song
  Is singing and saying still:
  " A boy's will is the wind's will,
And the thoughts of youth are long, long thoughts."
                LONGFELLOW
                (1807-1882)

1. See question 3 on " The Golden City of St. Mary ".
2. Which stanza do you like best?
3. Which lines are you likely to remember?
4. In what way does the atmosphere of this poem differ from that of the last?
Notes: page 196.

SONGS from THE TEMPEST

On page 103 a passage is quoted from "The Tempest". On board the ship, which was apparently wrecked, were Ferdinand and the King, his father.

Act I, Sc. II.

Enter Ariel, *invisible, playing and singing;* Ferdinand *following.*

Ariel *sings*

Come unto these yellow sands,
    And then take hands:
Curtsied when you have and kiss'd
    The wild waves whist:
Foot it featly here and there;
And, sweet sprites, the burthen bear.
    Hark, hark!

Burthen dispersedly—Bow-wow.

Ari.—The watch-dogs bark:

Burthen dispersedly—Bow-wow.

Ari.—Hark, hark! I hear
The strain of strutting chanticleer
Cry, Cock-a-diddle-dow.

Fer.—Where should this music be? i' th' air or th' earth?
It sounds no more: and, sure, it waits upon
Some god o' th' island. Sitting on a bank,
Weeping again the king my father's wreck,
This music crept by me upon the waters,
Allaying both their fury and my passion
With its sweet air: thence I have follow'd it,
Or it hath drawn me rather. But 'tis gone.
No, it begins again.

Ariel *sings*

Full fathom five thy father lies;
   Of his bones are coral made;
Those are pearls that were his eyes: 25
   Nothing of him that doth fade,
But doth suffer a sea-change
Into something rich and strange.
Sea-nymphs hourly ring his knell:

      Burthen—Ding-dong.   30

Ari.—Hark! now I hear them—Ding-dong, bell.

Fer.—The ditty does remember my drown'd father.
This is no mortal business, nor no sound
That the earth owes:—I hear it now above me.

                  SHAKESPEARE
                  (1564-1616)

1. This is the real elfin music referred to on page 141.

2. Some people say there is magic in poetry. If so that would account for the marvellous charm of these two songs.

3. There was other music on this island. See the speech of Caliban on the next page.

4. Lines 18-19. Compare these lines with Oberon's words on the next page.

5. Compare lines 23-28 with Clarence's dream on page 157.

6. Compare "Full Fathom Five" with "Call for the Robin Redbreast" (page 158).

Notes: page 197.

CALIBAN

Be not afeard; the isle is full of noises,
Sounds and sweet airs, that give delight, and hurt not.
Sometimes a thousand twangling instruments
Will hum about mine ears; and sometime voices,
That, if I then had waked after long sleep,   5
Will make me sleep again: and then, in dreaming,
The clouds methought would open, and show riches
Ready to drop upon me; that, when I waked,
I cried to dream again.

THE TEMPEST, III, 2

OBERON

      Thou rememberest
Since once I sat upon a promontory,
And heard a mermaid, on a dolphin's back,
Uttering such dulcet and harmonious breath,
That the rude sea grew civil at her song,   5
And certain stars shot madly from their spheres,
To hear the sea-maid's music.

A MIDSUMMER-NIGHT'S DREAM, II, 2

The Master of the Caravan

But you are nothing but a lot of Jews.

The Principal Jews

Sir, even dogs have daylight, and we pay.

The Master of the Caravan

But who are ye in rags and rotten shoes,
 You dirty-bearded, blocking up the way?   20

The Pilgrims

We are the Pilgrims, master; we shall go
 Always a little further: it may be
Beyond that last blue mountain barred with snow,
 Across that angry or that glimmering sea,
White on a throne or guarded in a cave   25
 There lives a prophet who can understand
Why men were born: but surely we are brave,
 Who make the Golden Journey to Samarkand.

The Chief Merchant

We gnaw the nail of hurry. Master, away!

One of the Women

O turn your eyes to where your children stand.   30
Is not Bagdad the beautiful? O stay!

The Merchants in chorus

We take the Golden Road to Samarkand.

THE GOLDEN JOURNEY TO SAMARKAND

At the Gate of the Sun, Bagdad, in olden time

The Merchants *together*

Away, for we are ready to a man!
   Our camels sniff the evening and are glad.
Lead on, O Master of the Caravan:
   Lead on the Merchant-Princes of Bagdad.

The Chief Draper

Have we not Indian carpets dark as wine,
   Turbans and sashes, gowns and bows and veils,
And broideries of intricate design,
   And printed hangings in enormous bales?

The Chief Grocer

We have rose-candy, we have spikenard,
   Mastic and terebinth and oil and spice,
And such sweet jams meticulously jarred
   As God's own Prophet eats in Paradise.

The Principal Jews

And we have manuscripts in peacock styles
   By Ali of Damascus; we have swords
Engraved with storks and apes and crocodiles,
   And heavy beaten necklaces, for Lords.

CALL FOR THE ROBIN REDBREAST AND THE WREN

Call for the robin redbreast and the wren,
Since o'er shady groves they hover
And with leaves and flowers do cover
The friendless bodies of unburied men.
Call unto his funeral dole
The ant, the field-mouse, and the mole
To rear him hillocks that shall keep him warm
And (when gay tombs are robbed) sustain no harm;
But keep the wolf far thence, that's foe to men,
For with his nails he'll dig them up again.

WEBSTER
(-1630?)

1. What is it that charms us in this little poem and makes it like one of Shakespeare's Songs?

Notes: page 197.

CLARENCE

Methought I saw a thousand fearful wrecks;
Ten thousand men that fishes gnaw'd upon;
Wedges of gold, great anchors, heaps of pearl,
Inestimable stones, unvalued jewels,
All scatter'd in the bottom of the sea: 5
Some lay in dead men's skulls; and in those holes
Where eyes did once inhabit, there were crept,
As 'twere in scorn of eyes, reflecting gems,
Which woo'd the slimy bottom of the deep,
And mock'd the dead bones that lay scatter'd by.   10

RICHARD III, I, 4

An Old Man

Have you not girls and garlands in your homes,
   Eunuchs and Syrian boys at your command?
Seek not excess: God hateth him who roams!   35

The Merchants *in chorus*

We make the Golden Journey to Samarkand.

A Pilgrim with a Beautiful Voice

Sweet to ride forth at evening from the wells
   When shadows pass gigantic on the sand,
And softly through the silence beat the bells
   Along the Golden Road to Samarkand.   40

A Merchant

We travel not for trafficking alone:
   By hotter winds our fiery hearts are fanned:
For lust of knowing what should not be known
   We make the Golden Journey to Samarkand.

The Master of the Caravan

Open the gate, O watchman of the night!   45

The Watchman

Ho, travellers, I open. For what land
Leave you the dim-moon city of delight?

The Merchants *with a shout*

We make the Golden Journey to Samarkand.
   (*The Caravan passes through the gate.*)

The Watchman consoling the women
What would ye, ladies? It was ever thus.
  Men are unwise and curiously planned.   50

A Woman
They have their dreams, and do not think of us.

Voices of the Caravan (*in the distance, singing*)
We make the Golden Journey to Samarkand.

JAMES ELROY FLECKER
(20th Century)

1. Lines 1-20. What are the merchants doing in these lines?
2. Lines 21-28. What new note do the pilgrims bring in?
3. Lines 29-36. Compare these with lines 1-20. What is different in the spirit of the merchants?
4. Lines 37-40. What new note is added here?
5. Lines 41-44. What is the merchant doing here?
6. Line 48. What is the spirit of the merchants here?
7. How would you read the last line?

Notes: page 197.

THE SHIP

There was no song nor shout of joy
   Nor beam of moon or sun,
When she came back from the voyage
   Long ago begun;
But twilight on the waters   5
   Was quiet and gray,
And she glided steady, steady and pensive,
   Over the open bay.

Her sails were brown and ragged,
   And her crew hollow-eyed,   10
But their silent lips spoke content
   And their shoulders pride;
Though she had no captives on her deck,
   And in her hold
There were no heaps of corn or timber   15
   Or silks or gold.

                                Sir John Squire
                                (20*th Century*)

1. What would be the effect if lines 5 and 6 ran thus?

      But sunset on the waters
      Was splendid and gay.

2. Lines 11 and 12. Whence came the content and the pride?

Notes: page 198.

NOTES ON THE POEMS

The numbers in brackets after the titles refer to the pages in the text on which the poems appear.

SAN STEFANO (11)

1. The metre here is very suitable to the story, suggesting the roll of the ship.

    It wăs mór|nĭng ăt St. Hel|ĕn's ĭn thĕ great | ănd gállănt dáys.|

    Note the prevalence of feet of four syllables. This is what gives the swinging, running metre.

2. Rhyme scheme: *a b a b c d c d*.

3. (a) We have lost the metre and rhyme (see above) with all the effects they have on the sound and meaning.

    (b) In the prose the ship is a dead thing sailed by men, and everything seems to go slower—we set every stitch she could carry—gave chase —overhauled her, hand-over-fist. In the poetry the ship is a live, eager thing, and everything goes much faster—she flung aloft her royals—she flew—she was nearer, nearer, nearer. Note the eagerness of the repetition of "nearer" as of a living thing.

    (c) In the prose we are reading a description of the chase. In the poetry we are in the *Menelaus*, feeling all the excitement of the chase, and thrilling to it.

4. The captain (Sir Peter) fears they may realise that he is trying to cut out the ship—may see the boats and fire at them. So in ghostly silence he takes up his position. Remember the time—the summer moon was setting. He sends his boats away, and then with a volley from over twenty guns he startles the citadel. The awakened gunners have eyes for nothing but the *Menelaus*, and at once begin firing at her. The smoke forms a screen for the boats, while the roaring of the guns drowns any noise, as they creep in, capture the French ship, cut the cables, slip out unnoticed in the darkness, and sail away in company with the *Menelaus*.

5. There are at least five:
    (a) The *Menelaus* leaving the harbour.
    (b) The chase.
    (c) The preparation for the attack.
    (d) The capture of the prize.
    (e) The *Menelaus* re-entering the harbour.

    Note the natural gaps between stanzas 1 and 2, and between 4 and 5.

THE SPLENDOUR FALLS (14)

1. The best way to make anyone hear the splendour of sound in a poem is by the splendour of your reading.
   (b) Rhyme scheme: *a b c b d d*, but if you add in the middle rhyme it becomes *a a b c c b d d*. Note that *b, b, d, d* are double rhymes.
   (c) and (d). There are many other points you may notice, *e.g.*, the vowels. I have taken only the simplest.
2. The echoes. Note how appropriate to both is the description in lines 7-10.
3. The horns of Elfland, the echoes, die away. But the echo which your personality rouses in the soul of another grows from year to year.

* * *

PIPING DOWN THE VALLEYS WILD (15)

1. In the last poem the line began with a weak accent which is here omitted.

   The splendŏur fálls ŏn cástlĕ wálls.
   Pĭpíng dŏwn thĕ vállĕys wíld.

2. Rhyme scheme, stanzas 1 and 4: *a b a b*.
   stanzas 2, 3 and 5: *a b c b*.

3. The child he sees is a spirit on a cloud, who tells him to pipe a song about a lamb, then to sing it, then to write it in a book that all may read. He does so that " Every child may joy to hear ".

4. Stanza 3 is complete in itself, ending with a period. In stanza 4 the period comes at the end of the second line, the third line beginning a new sentence which runs straight on—and, and, and, and—to the end of the fifth stanza.

5. The charm of this poem lies in its atmosphere of simple joy. Note the simplicity of the language and the repetition of the idea of joy. In stanza 4 he is enjoined to write his songs that all may share the joy. He is in such haste to do it, that he begins in the same stanza, running right on to the next, the succession of "Ands" leading to the triumphant last line. This will suggest how it should be read.

* * *

THE LISTENERS (16)

2. Rhyme scheme: *a b c b d e f e*.
   Alliteration: Line 4.

3. The traveller has knocked at the moonlit door and called, " Is there anybody there ? " and now stands listening in the silence. But he has startled the bird which flies up out of the turret.

4. The sudden flapping of the bird's wings startles him and he again strikes the door, louder because it is the second time, and perhaps because he is startled, therefore "smote". See lines 25-26. Compare line 7 with the corresponding one in rhythm, line 3.

> And hĭs horse ĭn thĕ silence champed thĕ grasses,
> And hĕ smote ŭpŏn thĕ door ăgain ă second time.

The slight irregularity in line 7 suggests the disturbed mind of the traveller. We are not sure whether to accent "time" or not. If we omitted "again" we should miss this effect.

5. The name of the poem is "The Listeners". If you make a decided pause at the end of line 8 you turn your audience into listeners, like the traveller, waiting for a reply.
Line 15. A listening line, therefore quiet, yet every syllable clear.
Lines 17 and 18. Let the voice go down the stair. Begin high at "Stood thronging", and go down tone by tone till you reach "the empty hall". It makes the hall seem very far down, and dark, and ghostly.

6. Lines 25-28. See line 12. The strangeness, the stillness is disturbing him (see lines 21-22) and he suddenly makes up his mind, hence "suddenly smote even louder". He is addressing the phantom presences (lines 13-22).

7. Line 28. What was said of line 8 applies even more here.
Line 31. An echoing line, therefore slow, to give time for the echo, and every syllable clear though quiet, for the still house; a most beautiful line to read.
Lines 33-36. If the silence is to surge softly backwards we must begin rather loudly. Note that the sound of iron on stone (line 34) would be clear and ringing. From there begin the diminuendo; do not suddenly drop to silence, but let it surge softly backward.

8. Note how indefinite even the definite things are: the traveller has grey eyes, but is he old or young, tall or short, fat or thin? He is just a traveller. This indefiniteness seems to add to the strangeness.

9. The mystery surrounding the story, rousing so many questions that are not answered, adds to the strange eerie atmosphere of the poem.

10. The dictionary says the atmosphere of a poem is the spiritual influence pervading it. Think of the feeling aroused, the effect on you as you read "San Stefano", then "The Splendour Falls", then "Piping Down the Valleys Wild", then "The Listeners"—that is the atmosphere. As it is the finest thing in this poem and can be obtained only by reading the poem aloud, we must watch how we read each line.

OVERHEARD ON A SALTMARSH (18)

1. Lines 1, 3, 5, 7, 8, 10-13, 15, 17-19.
2. The writer evidently does not see them, he merely "overhears". Note the name of the poem.
3. Where they would be overheard, not seen. This heightens the effect of the reading.
4. Is she teasing him and enjoying it, or is she just interested and astonished?
5. The Goblin is eager and petulant like a child wanting a toy. His tone rises steadily right through the poem. Note lines 10-13: "better—better —better". Note the effect of line 14, which adds so much to the glamour of the beads, in the Goblin's eager reply, line 15.
6. The word "No". It occurs four times and should be spoken differently each time.

*   *   *

TREASURE-TROVE (19)

1. This depends on how you read it. I read it thus: 3 3 5 5 3. Line 4 may have seven beats.
2. Green is the fairy colour. See "Thomas the Rhymer":
"Her skirt was o' the grass-green silk".
3. I think the third stanza and the third line of it. Note that in the first stanza the hill heids are "steep," and that in the fourth they are "grey."
4. Here you must choose for yourself.

*   *   *

THE FORSAKEN MERMAN (20)

1. No. But the title makes even the first stanza sad.
2. The repetition of "now" emphasises the time, as if it said, "It is time we were away, for now . . . now . . . now . . . now . . ." In lines 36-43 the repetition of "where" (six times) brings us back to the sand-strewn caverns, emphasising the fact that all these wonderful things are there.
3. I read them thus: Line 2 has three beats; lines 9, 11, 13, 19, 22, have two beats; the rest, four beats.

Rhyme scheme, lines 1-9: *a b a b b a a a a*.
lines 10-22: *a b a b c c d d e e b b*.

But to show how the two stanzas are linked together in sound they should be taken as one. The rhyme scheme is then *a b a b b a a a a. b c b c d d e e a a a c c.*

4. In lines 1-47 the poet gives us the atmosphere, and rouses us to sympathy and wonder, so that we read on with eagerness.

5. Here you must choose for yourself.

6. Our sympathy is perhaps more with Margaret. We pity the Merman, but he has still his children, and his love for Margaret, and he is not to blame in any way. But in lines 76-84 we see Margaret torn between her love for her life on earth and her love for those she has deserted. Lines 124-143, however, which end the poem, are full of the beauty of the moonlit shore and the love of the Merman for the one who has forsaken him. It is right that we should finish with the Forsaken Merman.

* * *

KILMENY (26)

1. The poem is much too long to quote in full. The following lines help to explain stanza 2:
   "When seven lang years had come and fled,
   When grief was calm, and hope was dead,
   When scarce was remember'd Kilmeny's name,
   Late, late in the gloamin' Kilmeny came hame!"

   Lines 14-17 merely emphasise how long it is since she disappeared. In line 18 the poet starts to tell us of her return, but stops in the middle to tell us how strange it was; how still that sunset in the late autumn, with the waning moon, and the cottage smoke like a little lonely cloud; why, even the firelight seemed eerie when
   "Late, late in the gloamin' Kilmeny came hame."

2. We should lose the whole effect given above, the waiting and wondering—the mysterious.

4. No. Line 25 expresses surprise and joyful welcome, but as they look at Kilmeny a feeling of wonder and awe comes over them, which should appear in the reading of line 32.

5. In "The Wife of Usher's Well" in Book II. You will find it again in "The Dowie Dens o' Yarrow."

6. No. She cannot answer the question in stanza 3. All she can do is to give the impressions summed up in lines 50-51.

7. Kilmeny had been in "The Land of the Spirits", *i.e.*, in Paradise.

THOMAS THE RHYMER (29)

The notes given with the poem are taken from "Highways and Byways in the Border", Andrew and John Lang, pages 217-219, "Come Hither", Walter de la Mare, page 550, and Scott's "Minstrelsy of the Scottish Border".

1. See lines 65-76.

2. The one tells us of the lady's dress, and her horse, the other of the lady herself. Which do you see more clearly?

3. La Belle Dame woos the knight and wins him. The Queen of Elfland "dares", challenges True Thomas, and wins him, lines 21-24.

4. See The Gospel St. Matthew, VII, 13 and 14.

7. The minstrel with his passionate love of beauty, lines 9-12; his reckless daring, lines 21-24; his outspoken frankness and his sense of humour, lines 69-74. "The tongue that can never lie" might not be too profitable in buying and selling at the markets, or in speaking to prince or peer or fair ladye.

8. In thirteen. In the old ballads we find very frequently this mixture of dialogue and narrative, the one changing abruptly into the other. See "The Dowie Dens o' Yarrow", "Sir Patrick Spens", "The Bonnie Earl of Murray" (first version). In the modern ballads in this book this old custom is followed, but generally the abruptness is softened—we are led into the direct speech—see "San Stefano", line 25, "Hervé Riel", line 16.

* * *

MORTE D'ARTHUR (36)

1. Lines 1-12. Here you must choose for yourself. For Lyonnesse see "Highways and Byways in the Border", Andrew and John Lang, pages 244-5 and 347.

2. Lines 16, 26 and 27. The addition rather retards the action, and tends to take away from the effect of the climax (lines 71-5).

3. Lines 28, 32 and 33. The prose Sir Bedivere is more matter of fact. The other talks more, perhaps feels more.

4. The prose here states the bald fact. The poetry shows us the scene, gives us its weird atmosphere, makes it live, and gives us the beautiful line 40.

5. For the reason given in note 4. Here Sir Bedivere gazes with dazzled eyes on the jewelled hilt sparkling in the frosty moonlight, and ponders what to do.

6. Malory's words suit his rather matter-of-fact Sir Bedivere. He hides the sword and hurries back. Tennyson's words suit the dazzled Sir Bedivere, who ponders what to do, hides the sword, and goes back slowly, troubled in mind.

7. See note 6. Each is certainly the better in its place.

8. Lines 61-4 and 71-5. With the exception of lines 68 and 69, which hardly seem necessary, Tennyson has added a very beautiful picture. Lines 71-5 (verse) give a clear and wonderful picture, though we have had part of it already, in lines 18-20 (verse): but lines 39-43 (prose) are so simple, so sincere and have such dignity that they make us feel the mystery more. We admire the picture in the poetry, we are convinced of its truth in the prose.

9. He is no longer troubled in mind. He has seen the wonderful sight and is in haste to tell the King.

10.
{ Poetry, line 33. "And lightly bring thee word."
{ Prose, line 6. "And lightly bring you word."

{ Poetry, line 16. "Thou therefore take my brand Excalibur."
{ Prose, lines 1 and 2. "Therefore take thou Excalibur, my good sword."

11. This is a fine example of blank verse.

*   *   *

AUTOLYCUS' SONGS (41)

1. I. The zest for life, together with a simple direct love of flowers and spring, untroubled by any theories.
II. As above, but here, especially, the merry heart—not merely the carefree, but the merry heart.

*   *   *

THE STRANGER (42)

1. Yes. In the fourth line he is very like him.

2. No. In line 20 he is not like him.

3. The poem begins in the spirit of Autolycus' Songs, but the laughter seems to be only "in his e'e". His heart is not laughing, at least not laughing merrily. There is too much criticism, and contempt for others.

4. I do not think so, in spite of line 18. The laughter does not permeate the poem. The spirit is much more akin to that of "For A' That, and A' That."

5. Yes. The whole poem leads up to this. The Stranger's contempt for wealth and comfort rises stanza by stanza, until he leaves us, walking like a king.

*   *   *

FOR A' THAT, AND A' THAT (43)

1. Is there anyone who for honest poverty hangs his head?—He is the coward slave.

2. The last two lines of each stanza contain a general statement which seems to sum up and round off the stanza.

3. The last two lines of each stanza. These ten lines sum up the wisdom of the poem with none of its bitterness, while lines 39 and 40 form a prayer in which all classes can join.

4. Yes. As each stanza rises to the expression of a great truth, so the whole poem rises to the expression of an ideal for all men.

5. They resemble each other in their criticism of and contempt for wealth, etc. But the Stranger is a king at heart, while the speaker in this poem is a fierce supporter of the dignity of honesty and the independent mind, especially among the poor. There is no laughter even "in his e'e," but there is a broad outlook on life, which leads up to a prayer for all mankind.

6. This poem lacks the gusto for life, and the merry heart of these songs, *i.e.*, their unthinking happiness.

7. See "Essay on Man", IV, line 203. Note the neatness and exactness of statement, and the balance of the one half against the other of Pope's line. It lacks the force and splendour of Burns' metaphor. The latter is certainly the finer poetry.

8. Goldsmith has put the point with great clarity and strength, but both he and Pope seem to be trying to teach something. "For A' That" is a song, and lines 25-8 have music and glamour besides clarity and strength.

*   *   *

THE VAGABOND and A CAMP (45) (46)

1. The change of atmosphere is delightful. The Vagabond has a certain self-sufficingness, and with him we seem to breathe the full joy of life.

2. Perhaps, but the Vagabond could not be the Stranger. We cannot imagine him going near any town, much less criticising the people in it. The critical spirit common to " The Stranger " and " For A' That " does not exist here.

3. Each delights in life. Autolycus' Songs paint the person who would make an ideal companion, and who would go whistling on cheerily alone if there were no one to go with him. But the Vagabond would not make a good companion—he does not want a companion. See lines 13 and 14. He is a

> " Bird of the wilderness
> Blythesome and cumberless ".

4. They would all be happy in " A Camp", but it seems the natural home for the Vagabond. He would never want any other home. There is the same delight in life, the same self-sufficingness in each poem.

*   *   *

From AS YOU LIKE IT (47)

1. This is the spirit of Autolycus' Songs. We are back to the merry heart, and that simple direct delight in the open air, and the sights and sounds of nature. Note that we are back to Shakespeare.

2. The song is sung by Amiens, one of the young men described by Charles. It reproduces exactly the spirit of the passage quoted from Act I. As a modern poet puts it:

> " What is this life if, full of care,
> We have no time to stand and stare ? "

3. Note especially the line

> Cóme hithĕr | cŏme hithĕr | cóme hithĕr. |

It is like the warble of a bird ; we feel he has turned

> " His merry note
> Unto the sweet bird's throat."

4. Jaques' song is a parody of Amiens' song and a criticism of the Duke's action in making his home in the woods, though his hearers take it merely as a joke, because they know the spirit of Jaques. When he rises to sing

he beckons to the others to gather round him. So when Amiens asks the meaning of "ducdame", Jaques' answer seems to apply to them, as they stand in a ring round him. "Ducdame" must be pronounced like "come hither"—hence, "dŭcdámĕ."

5. The first song, "Under the greenwood tree", we may call positive, the second, "Blow, blow, thou winter wind", negative. The first tells of the joys to be had; it seems to say, "If you love these things, come hither They are all here, and your only enemy will be the rough weather." The second song tells of the evils we escape if we "come hither". The winter wind may blow keen and the bitter sky freeze, but ingratitude and forgotten friendship hurt much more deeply. Hence the spirit of the first song is merry, glad, carefree; of the second, serious. It offers the consolation to be found in the free life of the woods for the evils of this life.

* * *

I WILL MAKE YOU BROOCHES (51)

1. The singer is going to make a palace with all sorts of delights for his lady. The palace is to be the green forest and the blue sea. If so, the brooches and toys will be the delights of the open-air life, the morning song of the birds, the stars at night. Note that he mentions the stars in "The Vagabond" and "A Camp".

2. You might spend days in the green forests, unhappy days when you were ill, or suffering, say, from toothache. They would not be green days in forest. Only when your days are full of the freedom and beauty of the green forests and blue sea do you think of them as "green days in forests and blue days at sea".

3. "White" here means not only clean, but beautiful. Think of the green forests and blue sea, the white foam on the river, the bright golden broom. The lady, too, is beautiful with her white skin. And what so delightful to wash in as the rain and dew?

    For it's dabbling in the dew makes the milkmaids fair.

4. "The Vagabond" and "A Camp". See especially stanza 3. Is this not the Vagabond, with a mate at last, in Camp?

Pictures from I STOOD TIPTOE UPON A LITTLE HILL (52)

2. To the ear—lines 4-5, 10-12.

   To the other senses—particularly lines 14-19, though in a way we feel them all.

   To the eye—the rest.

3. Here you must choose for yourself.

4. Again you must choose for yourself, but consider lines 4, 6-7, 10, 16-17,

* * *

THE DOWIE DENS O' YARROW (53)

There are many versions of this ballad. This one has come down to me in the old historical way. Nearly fifty years ago I learned it by heart from hearing my father recite it. He told me he had never seen it in print, but had learned it when he was young from a man who used to recite it.

1. Lines 5-8, 13-14, the brothers-in-law. Lines 9-12, 15-16, the husband.

2 and 3. The brothers-in-law are forcing a quarrel on the husband. They are in a tavern—it is "late at e'en," and they have been drinking.

4. When we read the words of the brothers-in-law there should be an aggressive note, and sometimes a note of contempt. The husband speaks in a dour, determined manner, giving the feeling that he is being forced into the quarrel and will make them sorry for it.

5. The brothers say that she was the bonniest girl in Yarrow at the time *when* she was married. The husband, who loves her, sees her as beautiful as ever, and says, "She's *aye* the Rose o' Yarrow." The two words *when* and *aye* make all the difference.

6. Lines 25-6 should be read cheerfully—he is trying to soothe his wife's fears; but the dour note creeps into lines 27-8.

7. The wife. This has been woman's heaviest burden in the past, to arm the man she loves and let him go out to face the danger, while she waits and fears for him. It could not be expressed more simply or more beautifully.

8. Fitz-James' speech is fine—brave—gallant. But in the ballad we have "the real thing". He sees clearly his hopeless position (line 50) and accepts it with grim determination and wonderful spirit. See the magnificent threat in line 46.

9. In the old ballads the audience were expected to know certain things, and so were not told. Thus we do not know who guid-brither John is.

10. See the note on the birk in "The Wife of Usher's Well", Book II.

11. In thirteen. See note 8 on "Thomas the Rhymer", (page 170).

* * *

SIR PATRICK SPENS (57)

1. As is the custom in the old ballads, we are not told. Their makers knew and thought that everybody knew. The old ballads are simple stories, simply told, for simple folk. Their finest quality is their absolute sincerity. The poet was telling what to him was a true story. We feel that he believes it, and we cannot help believing it, too.

2. 4, 3, 4, 3. *a b c b*.

3. We should of course lose the emphasis. But much more important than that, we should lose the music of the repetition, a simple kind of music loved by the people. This is one of the commonest characteristics of the old ballads.

4. See line 25. The following from Percy's *Reliques* may be of interest: "In the infancy of navigation, such as used the northern seas were very liable to shipwreck in the wintry months: hence a law was enacted in the reign of James III (a law which was frequently repeated afterwards) 'That there be na schip frauched out of the realm with any staple gudes, fra the feast of Simons day and Jude, unto the feast of the purification of our Lady, called Candelmess ' ".

6. Lines 41-42. See note 3, above. See also lines 57-8.
Lines 43-44. A wonderful description of a storm in two lines, the darkening sky, the rising wind, and the sea black with storm.

7. Note how each stanza adds a touch to the pathos. We have the guid Scots lords, the guid lords' sons, the ladies waiting for the lords, the maidens, "for them they'll see nae mair", then the wonderful last stanza that sounds like the tolling of a great bell. Somehow it sounds not only like the passing bell but also like a requiem, bringing peace after the storm.

THE SHIPWRECK (61)

1. This is much more terrible. In "Sir Patrick Spens" the feeling of pity seems to brood over the shipwreck, while the last stanza is almost like a benediction. Byron, on the other hand, is interested in showing the terror and might of the sea and the helplessness of mortals. From this point of view it is one of the greatest descriptions in literature.

2. Quite the reverse. Two stanzas further on the poet is humorously cynical about the drowned. The absence of pity in the writer makes the description all the more terrible.

3. Here you must choose for yourself, but note the alliteration in line 1, day, down; line 2, waste, waters; line 7, dim, desolate, deep. Note also in line 9 the word, "farewell".

*   *   *

THE BONNIE EARL OF MURRAY (62-63)

1. Stanzas 1, 4 : The sister of Huntly, who is erroneously supposed in the ballad to be the wife of Murray.
   Stanzas 8, 9 : Huntly.

2. Twenty-four lines. See note 4, below.

3. "He's ben to his bed" is a bald statement of fact, but "He's ben, and ben, and ben to his bed" is a piece of vivid description. It lets us see Huntly creeping towards his victim, the very simplicity of the language giving it an almost ghastly realism.

4. The author is interested almost entirely in the story, not in the characters. Hence there is no characterisation, and very little description. But this is the baldness of realism. The speaker takes it for granted that his audience know these great characters and need no description of them. See note 1 on "Sir Patrick Spens", page 176.

5. In the second version the author is interested only in the character, the personality of the Earl of Murray. He aims at making us feel how noble, how accomplished, how charming his hero is. He takes it for granted that we know the story. It forms a complete contrast to the first version.

6. Take the last lines of stanzas 3, 4 and 5. As they stand they form a climax. "He might hae been a king", he "Was the flower amang them a'", "He was the Queen's luve." We cannot change this order without spoiling this beautiful piece of construction.

7. In the first version the atmosphere is tragic, with a note of pathos at the end. In the second there is the glow of hero worship which seems to lift us above the tragedy, while the last stanza has an effect similar to that of the last stanza of "Sir Patrick Spens" (see note 7, page 176).

8. The first is a fine little tragic narrative, but the second is a song, a finished poem.

9. Here you must choose for yourself.

* * *

THE PIPER (65)

1. As the piper's music is certainly appreciated, the street is probably in either Scotland or Ireland, but the lighthearted gaiety of the people is Irish.

2 and 3. We might say that "Away" is positive. "Away, away" comparative, "Away, away, away" superlative. We should lose also the effect gained in the reading by letting the voice rise and drawing out the "ay" —as if the spelling were, "Away, awaay, awaaay". See also note 3 to "The Bonnie Earl of Murray", page 177.

4. The repetition of "and" gives the feeling of speed, of an eager gathering together.

5. In the age of gold people loved each other and all were happy. Mercer Street suggests a different age of gold (think of the meaning of "mercer") and yet it was here that music had its triumph.

6. Joyous, lighthearted, gay. "And all the world went gay".

7. The rhythm here dances gaily. Does the rhythm of the next poem dance?

THE LITTLE DANCERS (66)

1. The first word, " lonely ", suffices.

2. Because of the two words " dreams" and " soft." The sky " dreams," not " broods " or " lowers ", over the little street, which is not only secluded and shy, but is a " soft" retreat for the beautiful thing that is coming.

3. In the first poem the street is in full daylight with everyone rejoicing and dancing. Where are you to find the centre of attraction, where are you to place the piper ? But in this poem all around is dark, except for the flooding rays from a tavern window, and in this light are the Little Dancers.

4. " Sedately " and " grave ". How different from
   " And all the world went gay, went gay "!

5. " The Little Dancers " ; their happiness is too deep for them to be gay. When a person is most deeply interested, most entirely out of himself, he is not gay, but grave, " Grave with a perfect pleasure ".
   "Then felt I like some watcher of the skies
   When a new planet swims into his ken ".

6. The music rouses the hearers. They wish to express their joy in the rhythm, so they dance. The music has now almost become part of themselves. But they would not be so happy if they did not try to give expression to it in dancing. They have a double joy ; in the music, and in the full and free expression of the feelings rising from it.

7. The rhyme schemes go thus : (1) *a a b b b c c d d a a.* (2) *a b a b c d c a c b c d.* It is natural that the simpler poem should have the simpler rhyme scheme.

8. Line 2. Note the effect on the rhythm of the pause at " dreams ".
   Line 6. Note the effect of the two accents coming together in

   There to the brisk measure.

   Line 7 suggests the music, line 9 the dance, while line 8 by contrast makes us feel them both.

   Of an organ that down in an alley merrily plays,
   Two children, all alone, and no one by,
   Holding their tattered frocks, through an airy maze.

   Line 12. See line 6. Their eyes shining.

9. See note 7, " The Piper ", page 178. Yes—sedately.

THE CONTEST IN MUSIC (67)

1. The boys have no swords, but you see the left foot and shoulder come forward and the hands move into position for attack or defence.

2. There is no need to make a quarrel. There is one of long standing and they are equally eager for the fight.

3. The challenge here (lines 49-50) is an insult. There might be some question which would prove the better with the sword, but Robin knew he was second to none as a piper. Hence his confidence.

6. Lines 82-83. Note how insulting Robin's manner is. Alan's anger, lines 84-85, does not excite him: see the cool cleverness of his reply, lines 86-88, and again in lines 93-96. In line 96 there should be a pause, perhaps even a suggestion of a sniff after "piper", before he adds, "for a Stewart." Without these words, it was almost a compliment paid by one who felt himself the superior. With them it is simply an insult.

8. On what did Robin depend for his success? On Alan's keen appreciation of music. This is clear in line 101. Then in line 102 he calls upon Alan to judge his music, and plays the piece as he thinks it should go. But you cannot put your heart into a piece of music without being elevated above small things by it. And now in his joy in the music and gratefulness to Alan who has called it forth and approved it, he would like to lift his rival, too, above trifles, into the realm of music. So he turns to the noblest kind of pipe music, the pibroch, chooses one "peculiar to the Appin Stewarts and a chief favourite with Alan", and puts his whole heart into it.

10. Alan not only recognises that Robin is the greater musician, but he has lost his anger in his love for his rival's music. Surely nothing could be nobler or more generous than his acknowledgment of his defeat, lines 123-130.

11. (a) Lines 113-122 are to me pure poetry in spite of the fact that they are in the form of prose. See also page 132. Surely this passage also is pure and beautiful poetry though translated in prose form.
(b) In the preceding poems you have seen the effect of music on people in the street and on two little girls; here on two enemies eager to fight—a much more severe test.

ORPHEUS (72)

2. Wherever Orpheus played, plants and flowers sprang up, as if Spring with its sunshine and showers accompanied him.

3. Read line 10, adding the conjunction, "that", and the meaning and construction of the next two lines at once become clear.

*   *   *

REVERIE OF POOR SUSAN (75)

2. She was country bred and is compelled to stay in London. The song of the bird takes her back to her home.

3. In her reverie she is back in her home and her heart is in heaven. But the dream fades. See lines 13-16.

4. Line 5, and line 13.

5. In London the noise and the traffic might make the reverie, the daydream, impossible, but the silence of morning not only allows her to hear the bird clearly, but to dream undisturbed.

*   *   *

WESTMINSTER BRIDGE (76)

1. No. This is not a reverie. It describes the real beauty of London in the early morning sunlight.

2. Early summer morning, but the sun is well up. Note " steep ", line 9.

3. In the daytime the busy streets are in every way a contrast to the fields. But this morning they lie deserted, beautiful and calm in the sunlight, as if the spirit of the fields had penetrated into the city, while the sky broods over it " in the smokeless air ".

4. Wordsworth is the poet of nature, yet he never felt a calm so deep as here in the heart of the sleeping city, and even to him,
    " Earth has not anything to show more fair."

LONDON SNOW (77)

1. (c) Think of the snowflake falling. It does not come straight down like a drop of rain. It floats about, meanders, but always makes its way down. This is how it is falling in the poem. The lines vary in length from eleven syllables (line 1) to sixteen syllables (line 3). (Note that line 37 has seventeen syllables.) This suggests irregularity, but each line has five, and only five beats.

   (d) The rhyme scheme goes thus: *a b a, b c b, c d c, d e d,* and so on. Take the second group of three, *b c b,* and note that it consists of two rhymes, that the one takes us back to the preceding group, while the other takes us forward to the group following. It goes backward and forward like the snowflake, but ever goes on. You can write out the rhyme scheme for the whole poem by following this plan.

2. You waken in the morning and see the brightness on the ceiling above your head.

3. We are unaccustomed to the silence caused by the snow. Think how it deadens the sound of cartwheels on the stones.

5. Both men and boys wonder at the beauty of the mantle of snow in its first freshness on the town. The boys are going to school, the men to work. The difference lies in the suggestion of the burden of care borne by the men, though even it is forgotten in the bewildering beauty.

* * *

WHEN ICICLES HANG BY THE WALL (79)

1. (a) The scene is a farm in the country. Winter there, in Shakespeare's time, was very different from winter in London in the twentieth century.
   (b) Exclude the refrain and you find that every line in the poem except one (line 14) tells of the cold of winter or its effects. He is thinking of winter as it is, not of any beauties it may have.

2. Each is a series of short, simple, direct statements connected by "when" or "and". Read them, omitting every "when" and "and". It is interesting to see how simple and direct the construction is.

3. Lengthen out the "whoo" to suggest the owl's hoot.

4. The poem makes a striking contrast between the cold outside and the warmth we find within, where

           " Roasted crabs hiss in the bowl ", and
           " Greasy Joan doth keel the pot ".

To us within, the owl's hoot emphasises this contrast, makes us realise how comfortable it is. If we change "merry" to "eerie", we should lose the contrast. It would mean that the owl's cry was bringing the cold into the room, making us shiver. Note that in the poem "There was a boy" Wordsworth refers to the hooting of the owls as "Concourse wild of *jocund* din". We are told in "Love's Labour's Lost" that this song was "compiled in praise of the owl."

5. The beauty of this poem lies in its simple realism. It is so true to winter, so true to life, that we cannot help seeing the scene and feeling the bitter cold. In "London Snow" we do not feel the cold at all, because Bridges is thinking not of the coldness, but of the beauty of snow.

* * *

From FROST AT MIDNIGHT (80)

1. There are four main pictures.

2. The third is a sound picture, "trances" being the most effective word in it; those unexpected moments of silence when the blast dies down, seems to faint or fall into a "trance", and we hear "the eave-drops fall".

3. In the sound picture we have the suggestion of the roaring blast, then the trances of silence in which we hear the drops falling from the eaves. Now even this sound is silenced as the eave-drops are turned into *silent* icicles by the *secret* ministry of frost and are *quietly* shining to the *quiet* moon. Note that these icicles are very beautiful but they do not suggest cold as those do in "When icicles hang by the wall".

4. There are many fine examples. Perhaps the best is
   "While the nigh thatch smokes in the sun-thaw".

* * *

THE PARROTS (81)

1. It would make a fine stanza without the second line. Read it, omitting the line, and you will see. But we should lose just that touch of mystery, surrounding the beautiful picture as it comes before our eyes, which leads us to ask why he will never know. Lines 7 and 8 answer this question.

2. Surely. The very peculiarity of the words used, "shrilly" and "shriller", makes us feel how intense the green and scarlet are.

3. You will find this picture grow in beauty and become more real if you try to see it clearly. Think not merely of the colours, but of the white peaks, the black cedars, the green and scarlet parrots, and the setting sun. The word "against" in line 6 should help you in arranging your picture.

4. Does the poet mean that the parrots are fighting? Does he not merely wish to emphasise the contrast or strife of brilliant *shrill* colours, and of the shrill crying against the silence?

5. The second stanza adds (*a*) to the atmosphere of mystery, (*b*) the sound, the shrill crying—the first stanza is a silent picture—and (*c*) the thrill of joy at the weird beauty of it all.

6. Yes. The thrill of joy should be felt from the beginning.

*   *   *

TWO PEWITS (82)

1. The rhyme scheme of this poem is simply a series of *a a a*, for every line ends with the same sound. But take it as a rhyme scheme of words and we get this: *a b c d b a c b a c e f a d d*. Does not this erratic scheme suggest the flickering erratic flight (lines 7 and 10) and the unvarying sound at the end of every line the continuous, monotonous cry of the birds?

2. No. They will be white or black according as in their flickering they gleam in the moonlight or are seen against it. The colouring of these birds is mainly white and dark.

3. It is the moon, the crescent moon (line 14) which is riding the dark surge of the clouds like a little boat riding at anchor, and silently, because the only sounds suggested in the poem come from the pewits.

4. Probably the poet himself. He would look like one in the dim light.

5. The difference in colour. "The Parrots", at sunset, is full of brilliant colour. "Two Pewits", after sunset, has only black and white and various shades of grey. Note that this poem also has a touch of mystery.

6. Here you must choose for yourself.

7 and 8. Paint the picture leaving the pewits out. The white crescent moon riding the dark surge of the clouds in the after-sunset sky, the earth black beneath, a figure like a ghost, and silence alike in the heavens and on the earth—what is the atmosphere of this picture? Now in come the pewits like two happy spirits, sporting merrily under the mischievous sky, mischievous, because a spring sky changes so suddenly. Surely the atmosphere has changed entirely. It may not be the time nor the place in which we should want to play, but although the ghostliness clings to the scene and is increased by the strange monotonous call of the birds, yet the birds are happy, are sporting merrily. It is springtime and they are mating.

DUCKS (83)

1. Here you must choose for yourself.

2. It is only when you look for them that you realise how few there are. Lines 52-57 provide the only one.

3. Part III (lines 64-71) shows the need of humour if we are to see ourselves as we are, and to realise the greatness of God.

4. Lines 1-2. As God turned his mind from the making of " big things " to " fashion little ones " and so to making " comical ones "; so
   " From troubles of the world
   I turn to ducks."

5. Again you must choose for yourself.

*   *   *

THE SKYLARK (*Hogg*) (86)

1. No.

2. The poet is chiefly interested in thoughts aroused by the bird. In the last poem, " Ducks ", there was no doubt about the poet's interest in the birds themselves. From this it follows that we see the ducks and we do not see the skylark.

3. You must choose here for yourself. In this poem the rhythm is quite regular, in " Ducks " it varies.

*   *   *

TO A SKYLARK (*Wordsworth*) (87)

1. No.

2. See note 2 on the preceding poem.

3. To the Skylark group. The stanza is from Shelley's " To a Skylark ".

4. I think the rhythm of Hogg's " Skylark " is the more appropriate here, if we are to think of the bird itself.

5. Not at all. We all love to look at birds and let our thoughts fly with them, and in both poems the thoughts and pictures are beautiful

THE TIGER (88)

1. Admiration and fear blended, fascination, awe, wonder.
2. See Genesis I, 24 and 25. But you are not meant to answer these questions. They are meant to make you think.
3. The feeling of wonder as to who could make so splendid an animal becomes mixed with fear and awe as he thinks of the terror and the might of the tiger, till he asks, who " *Dare* frame thy fearful symmetry ? "

* * *

HERVÉ RIEL (89)

2. The entrance to St. Malo was through the Race of Blanchard, a passage of great danger. The pilots were afraid, as the warships were so large, the tide so low, the passage so dangerous. They knew that they would be held responsible if anything happened.
4. He is not one of the St. Malo pilots, and they, who should know, have declared it impossible to take the vessels in. Though he is a coasting pilot, Damfreville and his officers know him only as one of the sailors. If they burn the vessels on the beach, at least the lives of the sailors will be saved. How is he to convince the officers so that they will trust their lives and ships to his conduct ? And is France to be ruined when he might save her ?

    " 'Here's my head ! ' cries Hervé Riel."

5. Running from Cape la Hogue to St. Malo they were sailing due south, so the north wind was the best wind for them, and it still held to help them through the difficult channel.
6. The last ship passes safely through, and Hervé Riel hollas "Anchor!" Then up the English come, too late, as *they* have no pilot to steer them through, and they are too late to follow the French ships.
7. The French officers and sailors.
8. He had already gained the only reward he wished ; he had saved France. Damfreville had declared it openly before everyone. What more could he wish ? Why, leave to go and see his wife, whom he loved, and tell her all about it.
9. " Praise is deeper than the lips."

Browning published this poem in 1871, when the French had been crushed in the Franco-German War. He received a hundred guineas for the poem, and sent the money to the relief of the starving French.

LUCY ASHTON'S SONG and THE REPLY (96)

1. The "Reply" applies perfectly to Hervé Riel, but you appreciate it more when you read it after "Lucy Ashton's Song".

2. Stanza VII. Think of Hervé Riel as admiral leading the whole squadron through the danger to safety at the risk of his life, and so saving France, he a poor coasting pilot. Surely this was
   "One crowded hour of glorious life".

*   *   *

THE YERL O' WATERYDECK (97)

2. Think of the beautiful picture in stanza 8. The princess is standing near the skipper (see lines 33-44) and he has been so struck with her beauty, her hair driven "oot i' the sleet", that he has been gazing at her, forgetting that he has the helm.

3. He now wishes to marry the king's daughter, and so would gladly please him.

4. On the strength of the cable depends the safety of a sailing ship when in port or riding out a storm, and only now does he think it "ower weel made".

5. Lines 109-112. A man of weak character tries to appear strong, to hide his weakness behind his title of king. This brings the flash of contempt (lines 115-6) which shows the strength of the lady's character.

*   *   *

From THE TEMPEST (103)

1. (a) Lines 3-4 show the sailor's trust in his ship and his fearlessness. Note his fine challenge to the tempest; if there is just sea room, no rocks or dangerous coasts near, then, "Blow till thou burst thy wind."

   (b) Lines 12-13 show how clearly he sees that "The rank is but the guinea stamp." His words are at least as great: "What cares these roarers for the name of king?"

   (c) Line 16. Face to face with death and asked to remember whom he has aboard, he gives the simple, true, human answer, "None that I more love than myself."

OPEN THE DOOR TO ME, OH! (104)

1. Think of the subject, love leading to death; the atmosphere; how much the writer assumes we know; the mixture of narrative and dialogue; the wonderful third stanza; and the resemblance to the real ballad stanza. (See "Sir Patrick Spens").

2. This is also the real ballad manner. It gains in beauty as it is repeated. You find that you read the words "Oh, open the door" with more feeling each time. The lines from Coleridge are from "The Ancient Mariner". They express perfectly the loneliness of the sailor and the great stretch of sea, yet how few words are used! See also David's lament for Absalom, (II. Samuel, xviii., 33):
   "O my son Absalom, my son, my son Absalom! Would God I had died for thee, O Absalom my son, my son!"

3. I prefer the third.

* * *

TO ALTHEA FROM PRISON (105)

1. The former is simple, passionate, tragic—a real love poem.
   This is gallant, chivalrous, loyal, with a carefree, lighthearted, joyous note running through it.

2. Second stanza, Friendship. Third stanza, Loyalty.

3. Some such name as "Real Liberty", as this is the one idea common to all four stanzas.

4. A paradox is a statement that seems absurd or contrary to the truth, but which is really true. See line 26.

5. The first stanza.

6. See "Coriolanus", II, 1, 52-3.

7. Here you must choose for yourself. Compare the famous line,
   "When thirsty grief in wine we steep",
   with Jonson's lines,
   "The thirst that from the soul doth rise
   Doth ask a drink divine".

* * *

MARY MORISON (107)

1. No, this is not at all like an old ballad. It is a modern lyric, a passionate love-song.

2. The second stanza is generally considered one of the most simple, sincere, true-to-life pictures of the lover in all literature.

3. Here you must choose for yourself. For myself I choose the last two lines of the poem.

THE HIGHWAYMAN (108)

1. The sound of the horse's hooves. Compare with "How They Brought the Good News from Ghent to Aix", in Book II.

2. The repetition lets us hear the highwayman riding, as if we heard him approaching from a distance, along the "ribbon of moonlight over the purple moor," "up to the old inn-door."

3. In the daylight the wind blows the branches apart and lets in the light. Note Keats:
    "But here there is no light
    Save what from heaven is with the breezes blown."
  But at night the wind is "A torrent of darkness."

4. A crescent moon amid scurrying clouds.

5. Either 13 (lines 73-8) or 15 (lines 85-90). I think 15. From the beginning we feel sure of Bess. When she has given her life to save him, we wonder if he was worth it? The answer comes at once:
    "Back he spurred like a madman, shrieking a curse to the sky."
  Yes, he was worth it, and that completes our satisfaction.

6. Re-read lines 91-102. These stanzas are a repetition of stanzas 1 and 3. The poet suggests that these are the pictures that will live. Note that it is not their strife and sacrifice that live, but their love, and so the ghostly highwayman goes to meet Bess, who still waits for her lover. It is their love that lives and should live.

7. Here love seems to conquer not only the fear of death, but death itself.

8. They suggest how popular superstitions rise.

*   *   *

SILVER (114)

1. The first two words of the poem give the answer: "Slowly, silently".

2. Line 11. This line gives the only suggestion of sound in the picture; if the scamper of the mouse is the only sound, how silent it must be! Note that it is also the only movement suggested in the picture (except for the slow motion of the moon) which shows how still everything is.

3. This is a beautiful moonlight picture, silver-clear, with no suggestion of mystery as in "The Listeners"; a silent, still, untroubled atmosphere. Read "Moonlit Apples" by John Drinkwater.

SOME MOON PICTURES (115)

1. Look over this book and you will find many. Think for instance of "The Forsaken Merman", "Sir Patrick Spens", "Frost at Midnight".

* * *

THE RAIDERS (118)

1. If you go over the poem noting every example of internal rhyming, alliteration, and sounding words, you hear them all much more clearly when you read the poem again.

3. Every stanza in this poem is a blending of the real and the imaginary. Hence the success of the poem. Stanza by stanza, we become more convinced that it is a dream, yet stanza by stanza it grows more real until we almost wonder whether the last two lines are true.

4. We should lose just the effect referred to in (3) above.

5. We must give full effect to the splendid sound of the poem and the eerie mystery of the dream.

6. There is all the savage wildness of a raid, but it is softened by the eerie mystery of the dream. We feel this most in the last stanza, as the atmosphere has been impressing itself on us stanza by stanza.

* * *

THE FORAY (121)

1. The mysteriousness of the dream has gone, and with it something of the savage wildness. The atmosphere is brighter, more matter-of-fact. The men here are real men, who have comrades and wives or sweethearts. They are all real raiders, setting out gladly on their foray. The comparisons following, if the stanzas are read one after another, all help to confirm this.

2. The one confirms the other.

3. Compare his welcome to his "blithe Grey" with the feeling in the other.

4. Stanza 5 of this poem is full of gallant chivalry, especially the last two lines. How different from the last two lines of the other!

THE WAR SONG OF DINAS VAWR (122)

1. This is a song of triumph. The speaker relates the events in a matter-of-fact way that at times is humorous. He is not disturbed in any way by pity. See especially the last two lines.

2. By cutting off the extra syllable we spoil the run of the rhythm, giving a feeling of jerkiness to the lines, and we lose the effect of the double rhyme.

3. See lines 22, 24, "led off", "head off"; 25, 27, "bewildering", "children"; 26, 28, "swim in", "women"; 34, 36, "bemoaned them", "owned them".

4. You must read it aloud in your usual way to find the answer to this. There are three beats in the line, but the first and third in each line are so much more emphatic than the second that we tend to read the lines thus:

    The móuntain sheep are swéeter,
    But the válley sheep are fátter.

5. These are the only two lines in the poem which do not rhyme. Each has middle rhyme, and while all the other lines in the poem have three beats, line 39 has four. These help to give a fine sounding finish to the poem.

* * *

MACPHERSON'S FAREWELL (124)

1. He could take his place in any of the three: he could ride with the "wind from Lammermoor", he would be entirely at home in the Foray, and is full of the spirit of Dinas Vawr, if we exclude the cynicism of the latter.

2. "Jog on, jog on." A merry heart goes all the way—in this case even to the gallows.

* * *

PIBROCH OF DONUIL DHU (126)

1. Here you must choose for yourself. Stanzas 2 and 4 seem to me the fastest—perhaps because in stanza 2, lines 1, 5 and 7 end with "and", thus running on into the next, and in 4, lines 1 and 3 end with "when", with a similar effect.

WILL YE NO COME BACK AGAIN? (136)

1. It expresses a wish we have all felt, in language so simple and sincere that we cannot help using it whenever the occasion rises.
2. The wish is expressed three times, surely not in the same way. Line 4 would be a question with half its intensity and meaning gone, if lines 1 and 2 were omitted.

*   *   *

BONNIE PRINCE CHARLIE (137)

1. The Cavaliers were fighting for their king against rebels. There was no other king but Charles I. The Jacobites were striving to bring back " Bonnie Prince Charlie ", his great-grandson. Nearly sixty years before, his grandfather had been driven from the country, and now the Hanoverians were firmly settled on the throne. In both groups there is the same passionate loyalty. But in the Cavalier songs there is a light-heartedness, as in a cause that must succeed. See " To Althea from Prison ", page 105, written by a Cavalier poet. In the Jacobite songs there is a note of yearning that is almost pathetic, as if they were hoping against hope. As a general rule Cavalier songs are English and Jacobite songs Scottish.

*   *   *

HOME THOUGHTS FROM THE SEA (138)

1. Browning on a ship, knowing that there are places all around famous in English history, points out, one after another, Cape Saint Vincent, Cadiz Bay, Trafalgar, Gibraltar.
2. In each of these places, " Here, and here ", England had added to her fame and so helped him, an Englishman, proud of the greatness of his country. Compare his " How can I help England ? " with Henley's

> " What have I done for you,
> England, my England ?
> What is there I would not do,
> England, my own ? "

*   *   *

A BALLAD OF CAPE ST. VINCENT (139)

1. Campbell says of England, " Her home is on the deep," and Cunningham, " Our heritage the sea."

2. They are forgetting the fine ideal contained in the last three lines of the poem.

3. In the last three lines of this poem.

4. The third stanza is a piece of bitter criticism which breaks the solemn, reverent atmosphere of stanzas 1, 2, and 4. (From one point of view, it is a flaw in the poem, though I should be sorry to lose it.)

* * *

HOW SLEEP THE BRAVE (141)

2. Collins thinks of the brave men of all time who have died in defence of their country, thinks of the famous Latin line, " Dulce et decorum est pro patria mori ", and writes his little ode. It is simple, sweet, beautiful, and reminds me always, somehow, of the beauty of a marble statue. Binyon writes after the Great War, in which he has lost friends. Hence the note of yearning and personal loss, which is not to be found in the other.

* * *

THE REVENGE (142)

2. See prose, lines 90-95.

3. Here you must choose for yourself.

4 and 5. Tennyson's picture in stanzas IV, V, and VI is very clear and effective, and we are never likely to forget lines like
" And the little *Revenge* ran on thro' the long sea-lane between."
But the prose picture is equally impressive, and supplies some points omitted in the poetry.
(*a*) We see how close the Spanish fleet was before the English ships sailed out.
(*b*) We see the master and others trying to persuade Sir Richard to set his mainsail, go about and run from the enemy, as the squadron of " Sivil " lay to windward of him and there was no other means of escape.
" But Sir Richard utterly refused to turne from the enemie."
(*c*) We see Sir Richard forcing his way through the squadron of " Sivil," steering straight at each ship he met so as to ram her if she did not give way, but each in turn ran under his lee. He knew that if he rammed a Spanish ship, he would get no farther, but was just as sure the Spaniards would give way. At length, the *San Philip* came down with the wind and " blanketed " him, taking the wind out of his sails.

6. I prefer the prose, as it is so clear, so serious. At the same time there is a real spark of humour in it.

7. Here you must choose for yourself.

9. "Was hunted like a hare amongst many ravenous houndes, but escaped." A vivid picture, and a great tribute to Whiddon's handling of his ship.

10. Note especially prose, lines 74-80.

11. Stanza XIII, lines 5-7. I think these lines are a blot on a fine poem. The prose is noble, especially, "And that being dead, he hath not outlived his owne honour."

12. Here you must choose for yourself.

13. The rhyme scheme at the first glance seems to be $a\ a\ b\ c\ d\ e\ b$, but when we take into account the middle rhyme in lines 3, 4, 5, 6, it becomes $a\ a\ b\ b\ c\ c\ d\ d\ e\ e\ b$.

* * *

THE GOLDEN CITY OF ST. MARY (152)

1. Is it because it is "Out beyond the sunset", and seen or imagined in its golden light?

3. See note 1 on "My Lost Youth".

* * *

MY LOST YOUTH (153)

1. Is not the beautiful town of "My Lost Youth" out beyond the sunrise, coloured with the magic light of youth, as the Golden City of St. Mary is out beyond the sunset?

2. Here you must choose for yourself.

3. Surely at least the refrain, the last two lines of each stanza.

4. Is it not like the difference between sunrise and sunset? In this there is some of the eagerness and hope of sunrise, a quicker pace and rhythm. In the previous poem the pace is slower, with the calm stateliness and certainty of sunset.

Songs from THE TEMPEST (154)

2. If by magic we mean that effects are produced in a way we cannot understand, then of course there is magic in poetry. No one can explain why the rhythm and words of these two songs charm us as they do. In all real poetry there is this magic charm, and if you do not find it for yourself no one can show you it. Often you cannot explain why a line is your favourite. You simply feel it. It charms you.

6. See the quotation from Charles Lamb, given in the note below.

* * *

CALL FOR THE ROBIN REDBREAST (158)

1. See note 2, above. I do not know. I feel it. Note how simple and direct it is, like a child's tale, like

   " Come unto these yellow sands,"

   and with the same magic charm.

   Charles Lamb says, " I never saw anything like this funeral dirge, except the ditty which reminds Ferdinand of his drowned father in ' The Tempest.' As that is of the water, watery; so this is of the earth, earthy."

* * *

THE GOLDEN JOURNEY TO SAMARKAND (159)

1. They are discussing the wares they have to sell as if this were merely a journey for business. But there seems to run through these lines an undertone of excitement.

2. The pilgrims give expression to this. "In rags and rotten shoes", they yet have the courage to face the journey for what may lie beyond, " The Grand Perhaps ". This makes it " The *golden* journey to Samarkand."

3. The appeals of the women and the old man fall on deaf ears. The glamour of the adventure has now dominated the merchants and they take up in chorus the words of the pilgrims. See line 36.
   Compare with lines 49, 50, Shakespeare's song in "Much Ado about Nothing":

   > " Sigh no more, ladies, sigh no more,
   >   Men were deceivers ever;
   > One foot in sea, and one on shore,
   >   To one thing constant never."

4. A note of softness and sweetness and alluring beauty.

5. He expresses what all have been feeling, giving the real reason for the journey. This is confirmed by the words of the women:
    " They have their dreams, and do not think of us."

6. Triumph. They are away at last. Note the direction: " The merchants (with a *shout*)."

7. To give the semblance of singing this line should be intoned, every syllable clear.

     *   *   *

THE SHIP (163)

1. It would spoil the whole atmosphere of the poem. If you feel this, you have learned the meaning of atmosphere.

2. They have accomplished what they set out to do, and are content, as you are when you have finished satisfactorily some hard piece of work you have undertaken, though it may bring you neither money nor honour. They know the trials and difficulties they have had to face, and are proud that they have not failed.

INDEX OF FIRST LINES

	Page
A body cam' to oor toon	42
A piper in the streets to-day	65
A stark moss-trooping Scot was he	120
At Flores in the Azores Sir Richard Grenville lay	142
At the corner of Wood Street, when daylight appears	75
Away, for we are ready to a man	159
Be not afeard; the isle is full of noises	156
Bird of the wilderness	86
Blow, blow, thou winter wind	49
Bonnie Kilmeny gaed up the glen	26
Boot, saddle, to horse and away	135
Call for the robin redbreast and the wren	158
Come, dear children, let us away	20
Come unto these yellow sands	154
Do you mind rinnin' barefit	19
Earth has not anything to show more fair	76
Ethereal minstrel! pilgrim of the sky!	87
Farewell, ye dungeons dark and strong	124
Follow thee! follow thee! wha wadna follow thee?	137
From troubles of the world	83
Full fathom five thy father lies	155
Give to me the life I love	45
Good Monsieur Charles, what's the new news at the new court?	47
Heigh, my hearts! cheerly, cheerly, my hearts!	103
How sleep the brave who sink to rest	141
How sweet the moonlight sleeps upon this bank	73
In the elm woods and the oaken	74
"Is there anybody there?" said the Traveller	16
Is there, for honest poverty	43
It was a close, warm, breezeless summer night	116
It was morning at St. Helen's in the great and gallant days	11
I walk unseen	115
I will make you brooches and toys for your delight	51
Jog on, jog on, the footpath way	41
Just in the door, he met Alan coming in	67
Last night a wind from Lammermoor came roaring up the glen	118
Late at e'en, drinkin' the wine	53
Lonely, save for a few faint stars, the sky	66
Look not thou on beauty's charming	96
Methought I saw a thousand fearful wrecks	157
Nobly, nobly Cape Saint Vincent to the North-west died away	138

	Page
Now, Bill, ain't it prime to be a-sailin'	139
Now haud your tongue, baith wife and carle	128
Nymph, nymph, what are your beads?	18
Often I think of the beautiful town	153
Oh, open the door, some pity to shew	104
O Mary, at thy window be	107
On the sea and at the Hogue, sixteen hundred ninety-two	89
Open the gates	62
Orpheus with his lute made trees	72
Out beyond the sunset, could I but find the way	152
O what can ail thee, knight-at-arms	34
Pibroch of Donuil Dhu	126
Piping down the valleys wild	15
Slowly, silently, now the moon	114
So all day long the noise of battle roll'd	36
Somewhere, somewhen I've seen	81
Sound, sound the clarion, fill the fife	96
The beauty of Israel is slain upon thy high places	132
The bed was made, the room was fit	46
The clouds were pure and white as flocks new-shorn	52
The king sits in Dunfermline toun	57
The King was on his throne	130
The last of our steers on the board has been spread	121
The mountain sheep are sweeter	122
Therefore all seasons shall be sweet to thee	80
Therefore, said Arthur unto Sir Bedivere	38
There was no song nor shout of joy	163
The Spanish fleet having shrouded their approach	149
The splendour falls on castle walls	14
The wind it blew, and the ship it flew	97
The wind was a torrent of darkness among the gusty trees	108
Thou rememberest	156
Tiger, tiger, burning bright	88
True Thomas lay on Huntlie bank	29
'Twas twilight, and the sunless day went down	61
Under the after-sunset sky	82
Under the greenwood tree	47
When daffodils begin to peer	41
When icicles hang by the wall	79
When Love with unconfinéd wings	105
When men were all asleep the snow came flying	77
Will ye no come back again?	136
Ye Highlands and ye Lawlands	63
You know, we French stormed Ratisbon	133

38162

DUE